TAILS OF THE MIRACULOUS

The Magic of Animal Consciousness

Quantum Whisperer Series
Book 1

Tails of the Miraculous: The Magic of Animal Consciousness
By: V E Girard

This book does not encourage or endorse seeking interactions with wild animals.

All animals should be respected in their habitat.

Photography: Valerie E Girard
drvegirard@panharmonic.com

Cover design by Heidi Zin, Ojai, CA
zinheidi@gmail.com

First Edition 2023
ISBN 978-0-9898821-4-9

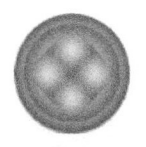

Published by
PANHARMONIC PRESS
Santa Barbara, CA

Dedication

To all my teachers,
both human and animal
who have inspired me
on my path to discover
the true nature
of the quantum field,
–which is love.

TAILS OF THE MIRACULOUS

The Magic of Animal Consciousness

Quantum Whisperer Series
Book 1

TABLE OF CONTENTS

My Initiation into the Miraculous

I didn't always enjoy miraculous connections with animals, I had to be initiated.

It was 2 AM. Clutching the helm, clad only in a bikini, I nervously lowered myself onto the captain's chair. I was the newly installed crew member aboard the Wave Dancer, a 36-foot sailboat. This was my first night of keeping watch for two hours as the ketch plowed through the moonlit ocean. Thankfully, the boat was on autopilot, as I did not know the first thing about sailing. My only job was to keep an eye out for other boats, visible by their faint twinkle of green and red stern lights.

As I settled into my navigational duty, I shook my head and wondered what I was doing, traveling down the coast of Mexico. Freshly out of chiropractic school, I had planned to sail from Acapulco to Los Angeles on their sloop with my best friend and her husband. A telegram sent to the Acapulco yacht club informed me that a cyclone had sent them packing back to Panama, delaying our meet-up by a month. Upon hearing my "Oh, no!" a handsome blonde Canadian seated next to me immediately offered an alternative adventure. "Why not sail with us to Costa Rica?" Huh, why not?

After meeting the captain and crew, and with no other choice in view, I jumped aboard. Now, here I was, sailing away from Los Angeles, with only a few dollars to my name. What would my mother say?

I took in a deep breath of the warm salt air. Suddenly, uncertainty about my future washed over me like some rogue wave. What the heck was I doing here on this boat with a bunch of strangers? Was I once again stumbling into a situation I had no control over? I already had several close calls traveling alone through Mexico. I did not dare think about how I would get back home. If I got home.

I looked skyward for my answers. The expanse of the Prussian blue night sky dotted with its swath of stars brought me back into the moment. The moon was waxing towards its full glory through silvery, distant clouds as lightning stabbed the 360° horizon. I shivered at the entire light display, complete with thunder surround sound. The beauty of it all relieved some of my trepidation.

Moments later, a flash of movement caught my eye off the rear starboard. I had company. Just four feet away, two dolphins streamed effortlessly on the boat's side wake, flowing in one synchronized movement. With knowing glances, they seemed to smile at me and convey the message: "Don't worry, we're here for you. Enjoy the ride." I could not believe that I was this close to dolphins! A surge of exhilaration blasted through my body.

Suddenly, I felt like I was on a mystical journey. The overhead stars twinkled in their eyes, enchanting me with a feeling that something magical was afoot. Maybe I had made the right decision to jump on board this vessel.

These beautiful sentinels stayed with me for the entire duration of my watch. Two hours at the helm flew by. What was this energy that passed between us? I wondered why they were there, but then let go to enjoy our ride together. Finally, with one flick of their tails, they peeled off, no doubt on their way to their next assignment. I now felt excited about my 180-degree change of direction.

The next morning, as we all sipped coffee together topside, I enthusiastically shared my experience of hanging with my new dolphin friends. My shipmates threw questioning glances at me and then at each other. "No dolphins on my watch." "Mine either," was all they said. My heart skipped a beat. Why only me? Did God send them? Was there a message in their appearance, and if so, what was it? I silently prayed that they would come again to fill me in.

They answered my prayers the following night. Within minutes of taking watch at an earlier timeslot, they again appeared. Of course, they stayed for the duration of my sailing duty, maintaining a perfect flow alongside me. Their presence now ignited something in me –my heart cracked open with a feeling of pure love for them. In turn, I felt their unconditional love radiate back to me. "Let go, let love" seemed to be the message. Bathed in moonlight, we flowed together on this beautiful ride. For the first time in a decade, I felt at peace. It was time to enjoy my Mexican adventure.

My fellow sailors turned out to be charming and funny. There was nothing to do all day as we cruised through the bright sapphire ocean but sun, swim, snooze, and share about our lives. I completely let go of pondering what lay ahead for me and was lulled into the beauty of every moment by the rise and fall of the boat's hull on gentle sea swells. Sometimes, my dolphins would round up two more of their own and cavort in front of the stern as I hung from the bowsprit, enjoying their synchronized play. They continued to school me in the art of frolic and being in the flow.

After weeks of sailing that included just one life-threatening stormy night, we anchored at Port Tapachula, nestled on Mexico's southern border. I could not continue the journey with my new best friends as I had no passport. Walking the streets of this quaint town, I suddenly realized I had no way to travel the 2600 miles back home. A wave of anxiety washed over me. I berated myself for not planning better. I took a deep breath, then remembered my dolphins. Let go and trust. Right.

On the last night of revelry together, we dined with a restaurant owner. Upon hearing of my plight, he paused momentarily, then offered to drive me the seven hundred and sixty miles to Mexico City. With no other possibility in sight, I accepted. At the crack of dawn, I climbed into the front seat of his small red pickup truck to set off on our two-day journey.

He insisted on driving the entire way over sometimes sketchy mountainous dirt roads. When it was too dark to drive, he procured separate rooms for us at the halfway mark. He brought me a delicious burrito to eat in my room. This kind gentleman refused to take any compensation. Once I was dropped at the airport, my remaining pesos bought me a ticket to Tijuana. It took my last dollar to pay for the trolly ride across the US border.

With my spirit renewed and inspired, I moved back to Santa Barbara to begin my chiropractic career. Over the following decades, I continued to reflect on my experience with the dolphins. What magical force called the dolphins to my side on those moonlit nights? Was this same force continually drawing me into intriguing experiences with various mammals, birds, reptiles, aquatic creatures, and insects? I eventually realized that these ofttimes-magical interactions were schooling me in the art of reading and interacting with the underlying field of energy that creates and binds our universe into one unified field of energy. These continuing experiences provided various lessons that progressively opened my heart to love and treasure all living beings on our beautiful planet.

Knowing our Earth now faces enormous challenges, I have vowed to make a difference by sharing my stories. May the following humorous, mysterious, and inexplicable tales of the miraculous inspire you to explore your connection to animals through this unified field and experience for yourself how delightfully conscious animals can be. They continue to enlighten me in a multitude of ways.

1

Discovering The Field of Connection

WHAT IS THE FIELD?

According to scientists, what we perceive as solid is, in fact, 99.999% space. What holds this .1% of matter in form? Is there a universal intelligence that created and formatted our reality? Are we separate in consciousness from the rest of this diversified creation? Is there a matrix that binds us all together in conscious awareness?

Scientists now say yes. They refer to this connecting force as the unified quantum field. I simply call it the 'Field.' This unseen energy matrix supports the physical reality we call life. It is most likely how humans tune into each other over distances, and all other living beings connect with other members of their species.

My interactions with the Field have often produced miraculous experiences that have enhanced my life in countless ways. But how did I first become tuned into this unseeable field of energy? It seems that the Universe had plans for me, one tale at a time.

STEPPING ONTO THE PATH

At 16, I had my first glimpse of the Field. I became interested in extrasensory perception (ESP) and experimented with sending thoughts to others through the Field. To my amazement, it often worked. While in college, I took a transcendental meditation course that initiated me onto a path of spiritual growth. It greatly facilitated my ability to focus on my studies. Two years later, I was initiated into a weekly meditation group that profoundly enhanced my personal growth and emotional healing. Above all, I was taught to always work for the good of humanity.

By my late twenties, I finished nine years of college and university to gain my chiropractic degree and settle into practice. I was immediately drawn to the "New Physics" emerging as the bridge between physics and spirituality. Books such as *Wholeness and the Implicate* by David Bohm, *Chaos* by James Gleick, Nick Herbert's *Quantum Reality,* and Rupert Sheldrake's *Morphogenic Field Theory* fascinated me. I attended every lecture I could by these authors to gain a deeper understanding of what mysteries lurked beyond the appearance of the material world. Initially, I grappled to grasp the full implications of their theories. Yet, over time, I intuited I had to *experience* the Field to fully understand its meaning in my life.

Many of these scientists' writings postulated that matter and consciousness are dual aspects of one perceived reality. That sounded very spiritual to me and ultimately promoted my continual inquiry into the intriguing interconnectedness of science and spirituality. I was drawn to studying various spiritual paths: Christianity, Buddhism, Shamanism, Esoteric Psychology, Indigenous medicine ways, Celtic practices, Hinduism, and more. Each excursion into one of these practices produced precious awakenings that enhanced my spiritual awareness. Delightedly, this also enriched my life and my ability to heal both humans and animals.

Stories from Findhorn, Scotland, also moved me. Findhorn was a high-producing farm that originated on formerly barren land.

They grew giant vegetables by communicating with the elements of the land. They also mitigated rampant gopher problems by calmly meditating with the varmints and sending them to move their habitat to neighboring empty fields. I wondered, could this interaction be the answer to my kitchen's ant invasions? As it turned out, yes! I spoke to the invaders and showed them pictures of me spraying Raid on the counters if they did not find their way out of my kitchen. The next day, they were gone for good. This led to more and more experimentation with communication with the animal world.

Over many decades, I experienced countless encounters with animals, insects, reptiles, birds, and aquatic creatures. These experiences bestowed me with invaluable insights into the intricacies of the interconnectedness of life; my understanding of the profound cosmic tapestry has been enriched beyond measure. I continue to express my deepest gratitude for the wisdom they have imparted to me. But what lessons have I gleaned from this planet's magnificent life forces? The answer lies in the following tales of the miraculous.

ANIMALS BECOME MY TEACHERS

Once I started having interesting occurrences with animals, another form of schooling beyond my college education began to take place. I was used to communicating with my pets verbally to train them to obey me. While this method got the job done, it failed to teach me how to understand what they wanted to convey to me. I had to learn to tune in and listen.

By learning to listen, I began to understand that all life is intelligent, including insects, fish, birds, reptiles, trees, and plants. It turns out, I had things to learn from them! Over time, I realized that their innate intelligence was the key to their survival and that of their species and our planet.

I eventually realized that animals connect to other members of their species through what Rupert Sheldrake calls the *morphogenic field*. This communication link within a species can occur over long, unsurpassable distances, as in the 100th monkey story. Another surprising teaching occurred as I witnessed animals expressing love and compassion for each other or even other species. I wondered if we humans could learn a thing or two.

Some of my lessons felt spiritual when I experienced synchronistic appearances of animals or witnessed healing expressions from animals. These incidents made me feel curiously alive, energized, and inspired. Eventually, interactions with domestic or wild animals opened my mind further to the possibilities that lay beyond what we perceive as our reality. I finally surmised that the universe was conspiring to teach me important lessons about energy via these interactions to enhance my healing abilities.

Ultimately, I learned to allow Universal Intelligence to guide my path as I traversed life's many expressions. When I was able to do this, I experienced ease and grace. The forthcoming tales offer intriguing illustrations of how my co-inhabitants on this planet came to enrich my inner awareness about the life force that binds us all together.

LEARNING TO CONNECT WITH NATURE

"Thoughts are things," said Napoleon Hill, "and powerful things at that when mixed with definiteness of purpose, persistence, and a burning desire." This idea unveiled the formula for opening the lines of connection between me and animals, birds, insects, and aquatic creatures. Using thoughts and clear pictures, in addition to some commands, allowed the pets and animals in the wild to register more clearly what I was asking of them. As you will see, I used this method to successfully interact with snakes, insects, and bats, not to mention more dangerous animals.

I also wanted to hear from the animals I encountered in nature or enjoyed as members of our household. Over my learning process, their communications became insightful, inspiring, and sometimes humorous. To effectively engage in this form of inner listening, I learned to empty my mind of thoughts and then wait.

Sometimes, they surprised me with a thought projection, as in the tale of the People Whisperer. With practice, I became increasingly intuitive as I tuned into their presence. It inspired me to be more reflective and open, especially while in nature. As you will see, this tuning-in became a true lifesaver at critical moments in my life. Opening my awareness to the Field also allowed me to facilitate more profound levels of healing in my practice.

After my sailing adventure in Mexico that I shared earlier, I fell madly in love with dolphins; my friends told me I was "dolphin crazy." I agreed. I began to think of myself as a dolphin as I pulled through ocean waters, training for triathlons. Some friends even suggested that dolphins might be one of my power animals. I had to ask, "What is a power animal?"

2

POWER ANIMALS

THE NATURE OF POWER ANIMALS

Many native cultures worldwide have observed the individual characteristics of animals, especially those in the wild. These traditions have attached meaning to the sudden appearance of these animals in their world, especially when these are noted in three different manifestations.

Indigenous cultures discovered tribal members' power animals through observation, dreams, outward signs, visions, shamanic journeys, initiations, and plant medicine. They observed that a tribal member's power animal could invest them with individualized traits, challenges, or strengths. Over time, these meanings have become consolidated into a spiritual data bank and are spiritually universal. Each animal embodies a lesson, often referred to as their medicine. For instance, dolphin medicine offers a balance between mind and soul because of their high intellect and intuitive aptitudes.

The Western world has embraced the spiritual concept of power animals as they appear in dreams, meditations, and journeys. Carl Jung addressed this notion by asserting that the appearance of specific animals in our waking lives or dreams has significance in determining emerging issues in our lives.

Various books have been written about power animals. Card decks depicting animals and their proposed spiritual meaning offer possible guidance to the spiritual seeker. My long-time reference has been the Medicine Cards book and tarot deck by Jamie Sands and David Carson. Other offerings provide insight into indigenous observations regarding the interplay between animals and their human counterparts. These cultures existed long before their subjugation by European invaders and had to live in balance with their environment to survive. It may be time to learn from them.

HOW TO DISCOVER YOUR POWER ANIMAL

There are several different ways to discover your power animal.

First, take note of those animals you have a natural affinity for. Perhaps you care for them in your home or engage with them in the wild. Then, notice if an animal's appearance in your life enkindles an energy boost or happens at an auspicious moment. Perhaps they appear several times in a row. Let this arouse your curiosity.

Some seekers employ spiritual ceremonies to discover and engage with their power animal. These practices allow kinesthetic access to the psyche to encounter long-repressed memories and emotional states. Burning sage or Palo Santo is often used to initiate a journey of discovery. A steady drumbeat or the deep resonation of a gong may be employed to nudge practitioners out of their "monkey mind" of incessant thinking. Some use various forms of plant medicine to intensify their deepening into the psyche. Imbibing a warm cacao drink may also enhance the inward journey by opening the heart center. All these modalities facilitate the release of the everyday world to experience the innate wisdom of the psyche and the Soul.

I knew nothing about power animals when I participated in my first shamanic practice. I had assembled a group of women meditators to camp in Joshua Tree, a gorgeous desert area east of

Los Angeles. While there, we joined forces with a friend's circle of women gathering to participate in healing ceremonies from various indigenous paths.

We pitched our tents among the giant boulders at my favorite campsite. The days were lusciously warm as we hiked the desert floor, searching for short-lived wildflowers. The nights were edging out of chilly winter temperatures.

On our last night together, we gathered in a clearing rimmed by the silhouettes of outlying Joshua trees; a majestic full moon rose over the eastern horizon. The day's warmth radiated up from the sandy floor, and an angelic formation of cloud cover filtered the full bloom of the moon's radiance.

We spread our blankets, each finding our place in the circle. My friends laid out their spirit items: drums, crystals, feathers, abalone shells with burning sage or smoldering sweetgrass. The desert offered its silence. Within moments of settling in, my mind and body were attuned to the collective intent of acquiring relevant wisdom for our spiritual paths.

Two practitioners faced each of the Four Directions: East, South, North, and West and invoked their presence into our circle. They offered prayers to the ancestors of the land, Mother Earth, and Father Sky, and finally to the Sacred Oneness of All. As I listened quietly, I felt something stirring within me.

The leader of our circle began to beat the drum, one solid beat after another. I soon fell into a deep trance. Without directing my thoughts, I suddenly found myself freely maneuvering underwater in a tropical ocean, possibly the South Pacific. It took me a few moments to realize I was a dolphin! I was strong and free, feeling at ease in my dolphin body.

During my aquatic maneuvering, I telepathically communicated with other dolphins and whales over great distances. It was a thrilling, masterful experience. At one point, I was hovering over my dolphin body, observing that one side of my brain was active while the other side of the brain was resting, perhaps asleep. Over time, the two sides of the brain switched functions. When I wasn't 'sleeping,' I effortlessly used my powerful body to flow in my reality medium, the ocean. The whole experience was ecstatic, profound, and life-changing.

When the ceremony was complete, I relayed my experience to the group. They suggested that 'dolphin' was one of my power animals! This explained my mystical connection to them on my sailing trip along the coast of Mexico.

When I returned home from the desert, I pondered how humans embody aspects of the animal world. It wasn't difficult to see the influences. "She's owlish," "He's bullish," "She's like a wild horse," and "That's catty." Sometimes, we use these references in a derogatory manner. Yet each power animal has its strengths as well as challenges.

The essence and influence of power animals exist perpetually on the quantum within their morphogenic fields. Once you discover your power animals, you may call upon them for guidance in challenging moments. Understanding the unique gifts afforded by your power animal attunes you to a primordial aspect of yourself. It is both grounding and empowering. Some websites (listed in the appendix) allow you to explore your possible power animals. You may also discover your power animal while participating in your own personal healing ceremony. Listening to a recorded drum beat or resonating gong with the intention of meeting your power animal may be the perfect invitation for your power animal to make itself known.

Many teachers across the United States offer Medicine Way workshops, following the work of Hank Wesselmann, Michael Harner, or Sandra Ingerman. Or, pick up the Power Animal or Medicine Cards deck, choose a card intuitively, and discover a power animal's message for you.

MEDIATORS OF POWER ANIMALS

A cherished soul sister who initially acquainted me with my power animal in the desert has guided many soul seekers to discover their power animals. In times past, when I journeyed with her via drumbeat, I was introduced to my other power animals: the cougar, the red-tailed hawk, and the owl. Since then, the appearance of these animals in my life has often relayed necessary messages regarding my life focus at critical moments.

Through several of these ceremonies, I realized my heart and soul yearned to maintain a connection to these animal influences for the archetypal strengths that they offered. In addition, these experiences markedly enhanced my connection to all animals. I began to perceive the spiritual aspects of all beings on Earth. Even as I maintain my bond with owls, red-tailed hawks, and cougars, more recently, I have developed a strong affinity with Bear medicine as I have become Mama Bear to several younger women, of whom I feel very protective.

It has been incredibly exhilarating to experience interactions with my power animals in the wild. I regard these experiences as sacred gifts from Spirit. Their appearances gave me a needed boost at challenging moments in my life. As with all wild animals, I mindfully afford them the respect they deserve in their habitats.

If an animal appears out of nowhere, especially in unusual settings, it may signal you to reflect on the meaning of its appearance in your life. This perspective must be respected as a gift from the indigenous people of the world, who honored all manifestations of life through their ceremonies and daily living. May we all be inspired to do the same to bring balance to our world.

3

THE FIELD THAT CONNECTS US

NATURE CONNECTS US TO THE FIELD

The indigenous people of yore had to engage with nature and all its elements to survive. They learned to tune into and sense whatever messages were offered by their natural surroundings. Their leaders consulted and communed with the Field as a natural form of spiritual guidance. They connected to their earthly co-inhabitants, calling them 'plant people,' 'four-leggeds,' and 'winged ones.' They afforded these aspects of nature respect for the contributions they provided to their survival, only taking what was needed, when it was needed. Studying their ways of living has inspired my love of the natural world and its variety of inhabitants.

Nature is readily available in urban settings via parks, lakes, trails, and beaches. Backyards are often brimming with bees, bugs, bats, and birds, all part of Nature's balance. Why be in nature? The natural world energizes and grounds us. It promotes a quieting of the mind. This then allows us to tune into the matrix that holds this fascinating cosmos together. This opens the possibility for connection and communication with the variety of life forms on the planet.

When life's minutia burdens me, I head to a park, beach, or hiking trail to ground, relax, and open to the secrets that nature is willing to share with me. While there, my interactions with any life forms gift me with a direct experience of our interconnectivity. These experiences enrich my life by assuring me that we are not separate from the mysterious force that links us together. This enhances my spiritual evolution. The real bonus is connecting with myself and my purpose in this lifetime.

MY SECRETS OF CONNECTING

The first secret is to be open to engaging with the animal world in all its various environments. In my interactions with the many benign and dangerous co-inhabitants of this planet, I realized how aware they truly were. A thought or feeling passed between us, often creating an intriguing outcome. When I doubted the authenticity of my experience, a similar incident occurred soon afterward. This is well illustrated in my two different encounters with rattlesnakes. The universe made sure I received the gift of the lesson.

So many miraculous tales have occurred with my pets, especially when we spent quality time together at home. They continue to school me in the art of connecting with the natural world. Therefore, practice with the animals you love dearly, whether at home or in the wild. They often have something to say to you and your heart. Ask them questions. Listen inwardly for their possible retort with your 'quiet mind.' By the way, cats will usually not respond immediately. It takes minutes for them to translate our human thought to 'feline.' An example happened last night.

I was at a friend's house, engaging in a beautiful evening of lively conversation. As I lounged on their couch, I spied two of their black cats sneaking through the sliding glass door and into the kitchen, scouting for their dinner. I adore black cats, so I called out to them to come over. My friend said they were shy and generally did not come to strangers.

Good time to experiment!

I silently reached out with my thoughts to the less shy male cat to "Come, get a pet." I visualized the manifestation of this request several times before returning to our after-dinner conversation. Several minutes later, the male cat strode to a nearby chair and plopped down. He was playing hard to get and would take his sweet time!

However, the shy girl registered my invitation: free pets! She slinked over to my end of the couch and nudged my dangling fingers as they twittered my invitation. Within minutes, she was contentedly seated on my lap, where she lingered for head scratches and tail massages. Then, Mr. Casual loped over for his pet therapy, and he, too, found his way onto my lap. Once both felines were well-groomed, they jumped down and sauntered to the bedroom for bedtime. Yes, I was smugly thrilled.

The secret? Engage their attention with a clear picture, maintain an open heart, and employ casual patience. You will be rewarded!

Not every animal will be receptive to your thoughts and requests. I've been trying to strike a deal with the mischievous crow that often snatches my cat's leftover food, hoping that by offering him some cat kibble, he would bring me a shiny gift in return. However, he remains uninterested, knowing well that he can always beat me to the bowl of leftovers. Nevertheless, I'm still hopeful for that long-awaited present.

If you are venturing into nature via hiking, camping, or backpacking, approach all animals with the respect they deserve. You are in their space. It is your responsibility to preserve their habitat. If possible, enhance their well-being as I did in several of these following tales. Most importantly, keep safe and leave the backcountry better than you found it.

ANIMALS REGISTER OUR THOUGHTS

In the many years I have been connecting with domestic and wild animals, I have often witnessed their ability to respond to my thoughts. Some interactions happened without my direct intention to communicate with them. At other times, I employed experiments at other times to see if an animal would react to my projected thought to them. Their ability to respond often corresponded to how centered and attuned to the Field I was at that moment. This is often related to my emotional state and my ability to 'just be.'

Over the years, our dogs and cats got more 'tuned in' as they spent time in our household; seven years seemed the tipping point. The dogs are more food-oriented when it comes to tuning in to us. The mere thought of retrieving any form of meat from the refrigerator gets them wrangling their way into the kitchen. When I am at the cottage on the East Coast, I experiment to see if the dog next door can energetically hear my thoughts "to come and get a treat." Even as I write this, she is scratching at the front door with her familiar whine for treats.

INTERSPECIES COMMUNICATION

What allows domestic to register to our thoughts and intentions and respond accordingly? What allows animals to interact with members of other species, safely and compassionately? Why have animals come to the rescue of humans, who they usually avoid? Why have wild animals sought out humans to help them when they normally steer clear of them? Each of these questions has arisen in my desire to understand how the quantum field influences the natural world.

To discover the answers to these questions, I was willing to tune into the universal Field that connects us all. This was accomplished by quieting my mind and learning to listen. It took practice, patience, and a willingness to experiment. Hopefully, the upcoming stories will inspire you to "tune into the space between the molecules" so that you experience your own tales of the miraculous.

4

THE WILD, AT YOUR DOORSTEP

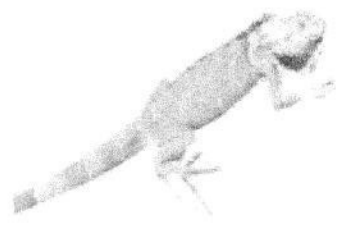

LIZARD LOVE

Sometimes, the wild comes right to your doorstep. I consider this a sweet blessing for the day.

I have loved lizards in all shapes and sizes since I was a little girl: chameleons, blue belly racers, or the much sturdier alligator lizards that liked to bask in the summer heat on warm rocks. As a youth and adult, I always wanted them to like me as well. I imagined that they were smiling at me from their rocky perches. I especially hoped they would want me to pick them up and pet them. Most of the time, they would scurry away as I reached for them with an eager palm. This love of lizards continued into adulthood.

One summer day, I was called to our doorstep to observe the tiniest baby lizard imaginable. My immediate intention was to prevent it from coming into the house (because of one particular cat who had yet to learn about co-existing with lizards). As I attempted to steer it away from the front door, it crawled onto my hand, continuing onward to my index finger. Even as I moved down the steps to escort it to a more hospitable environment, it remained in place on my hand. "Finally, a lizard that loves me," I thought.

I carefully lowered myself to the bottom step and held my palm to the light, marveling at this wee one's perfection. As I talked to it, its eyes opened, appearing to look right into my presence. Even as I took a phone call, it crawled up my arm and eventually took up residence on my back. We both seemed content as we co-existed in our unified field of energy. At that moment, I reflected that I hoped that one day, humans could also find a way to co-exist with those who appeared different.

Even as I eventually freed my tiny friend to go a-wandering in the fragrance of the lavender bush, I knew it understood my spoken words. In those precious moments, we were but one.

KNOWING IS BELIEVING

But what, exactly, is knowing? It is a much-honored gift that one may be born with or acquired with meditation and other spiritual practices. Inner knowing is clear cognition of information without hearing, seeing, or reading. Something is understood without external input. Often, knowing comes without pictures, words, or sounds; only an ever-so-slight vibration is registered throughout the body. I have had this gift since I was young, but I only realized it in my early twenties.

A new friend in my life gave me my first massage. When I got off the table, I knew that I would be good at giving massages. I did not have the funds to attend massage school. Not to worry, the Universe had other plans for me. Days later, a new acquaintance asked if I knew anyone who could give her a massage. I paused, then replied, "Yes, me!"

I borrowed my other friend's massage table and administered a full body massage to this acquaintance. I could sense and feel when I was hitting all the right spots. She shared afterward that she was delighted with her treatment. From then on, I began acquiring clients and intuitively learned from each session I offered. This funded my chiropractic schooling but, more importantly, taught me a great deal about healing the body. In addition to doing bodywork through my college years, a friend and I started a local massage school to share our knowledge with students and lay people in the community.

Some 40 years later, I still experience the tingle of knowing when working on people. Even more, sentences float through my subconscious that I then share with those I am working on. Every session has the potential to teach me something about healing.

Are you interested in becoming more intuitive? The video Developing Your Intuition may be found on YouTube @QuantumWhisperer.

CONNECTION HAPPENS IN THREE'S

Animals' visitation can be magical and inspiring, especially when they happen several times in close proximity. This form of synchronicity inspires me to ponder what message or inner guidance is being presented to me. Years after my experience with the tiny lizard on our doorstep, I walked up our driveway on a beautiful spring day, and my eye fell upon one of the rocks that line our front garden. There, perched on a smooth sandstone rock, was another tiny baby lizard. I gazed upon it from afar, then wondered aloud if it would let me hold it. I quietly took several steps toward the lizard, then stopped. It did not seem afraid of this giant form looming over it. Yet two more steps, and it scrambled away in the blink of an eye. I was a wee bit disappointed at my lost opportunity. I said out loud to the Universe, "I just want to hold a baby lizard again!"

Several hours later, I walked out to our backyard patio and stooped to retrieve one of the empty dog bowls for the four-legged's dinnertime. Much to my delight, a tiny baby lizard appeared stuck in the basin of a dog bowl. I stopped and stared. I could not figure out how this lizard got into the bowl since the stainless-steel walls of the dog bowl flared out, seemingly making it impossible for such a tiny creature to climb up the three-inch-high walls and over into the bowl. I looked at a nearby cement wall and imagined it taking a running leap off the top of the wall to land perfectly in the center of the dog bowl, four feet down. (Not likely.)

No matter, I thought, I must rescue it. I extended my palm just in front of it. Immediately recognizing its unimagined savior, it climbed aboard. My heart thrilled that this most diminutive creature would trust my hand, my heart, and me.

I brought it to my face and peered lovingly into its eyes. The lizard's gaze met mine, and I was in love. "What were you doing in that bowl?" I inquired. No answer, just an expression of trust as its little head tilted from side to side, sizing me up.

"I think it is time you go live in our luxury suite." I purred. I walked up the steps into our meditation pavilion and sidled over to the indoor tropical garden, laced with beautiful plants, crystals, candles, and all forms of sacred statues. Smooth small pebbles line our tropical indoor garden. As I called for a camera, the wee one did not move on my extended palm. While waiting, we chatted about bugs and other resident lizards.

I was able to take a few selfies with my tiny friend. Still, the lizard seemed content in my outstretched palm. After our photographic session, I gently lowered my hand onto the garden's pebbles, scattered amidst the delicate green ferns. The little lizard seemed to contemplate her next move. Finally, she scrambled off my hand and into the arms of a welcoming plant, ready to explore her new surroundings. The joy I experienced from our encounter lasted throughout the evening.

That was a wonderful gift from the Universe, but something interesting happened two days later. Another slightly larger lizard appeared again in the dog food bowl. I could not believe my eyes, and this time spent a few moments attempting to engineer how such a small lizard could find its way into--but not out of--the bowl.

I again picked up this lizard in my palm and carefully moseyed up the wooden steps to the indoor garden for our requisite chat. I wondered if it was the same lizard who had grown a bit over the last few days. When I lowered my hand again, however, my reptilian friend jumped off, perhaps too eagerly, knowing I would always be there if needed.

There were three lizard sightings in total, each giving me a gift of connection to the energy field that exists beyond the normal bounds of the world of density.

What allows these charming occurrences to manifest? I surmised that it was my willingness to align with the Field, sometimes just by being in nature or practicing inner silence. When I do this, magic invariably happens, especially when I am in that state of openness and quietude.

FURTHER SYNCHRONICITY FOR GOOD MEASURE

Years later, on a warm summer day, I visited two friends whose home included a lovely swimming pool up in the foothills of Santa Barbara. We began a rather erudite conversation encompassing our mutual interest in the physics of spirituality. We opened our conversation with a discussion centered around the idea of the Field. Lounging poolside, we noticed a large red-tailed hawk land in the East atop a telephone pole just barely a stone's throw away. Shortly after, a red-shouldered hawk appeared atop a short, lopped-off tree in their orchard just to the West. Seeing two hawks at once was a new occurrence for my friends, and we took it to mean that our mutual interests in the Field produced an enlightening conversation, as hawks are considered the messengers of Spirit.

We reminisced about our various encounters with animals in the wild. I excitedly shared my experiences with the tiny lizards that impossibly appeared in the dog's bowl. As I recounted the stories, I shared that I remained puzzled about how those lizards appeared inside the same bowl on two occasions. I expressed my hope that it would happen again.

Not two days later, I walked out to the stone patio only to find that a baby lizard had landed in the same dog bowl, facing the same direction as the other two lizards! I was elated and hoped that I would get to share some time with this tiny one.

I picked up the bowl, walked again to our meditation pavilion, and tilted the bowl. The little one walked onto my palm. It remained motionless, looking at me with lizard curiosity. I snapped a selfie of me almost kissing it. It took a bit of time for me to finally convince it that it would be safe to move to one of our lovely fairy ferns, with a much better possibility of finding a tidy snack! It gingerly climbed off my extended palm into its new environment, disappearing into the wilds of awaiting houseplants.

While many people are scared or squeamish about the reptilian world, I have always found a peaceful delight in their presence on those rare occasions of an encounter in the wild, or at least on my doorstep.

5

ANIMALS AS TEACHERS

SKUNKS: FRIENDS IN THE FIELD

We have often entertained skunks in our yard, considering them "outdoor pets." Of course, we also desperately discourage our enthusiastic dogs from running outside to chase them. When I encounter skunks, usually at night, I call out to them to "move along now" with an affectionate yet cajoling voice. Thus, they never feel threatened and soon find their way out of the yard.

One warm summer night, one of my classes was gathered in the OM Pavilion, a large deck behind the house covered with a large tent. We were enjoying a moment of silence. I sensed something moving and opened one eye to glance to my right; three feet away, a determined skunk was trundling up the steps to join us. I paused momentarily, then quietly said, "Skunky, best move along." Skunky raised his head to look at me, reconsidered his advance, turned, and headed down the stairs to saunter out of the yard.

Another night, some students and I gathered again in our pavilion. Halfway through our meditation, we heard an unusual sound. We stopped, opened our eyes, and turned to see its origin. Our 'pet' skunk was drinking from the dog's water bowl. Close by, our female cat was calmly gazing upon Skunky.

As if on cue, one of our dogs, Gracie, poked her head out of the back door and, fortunately, drew up suddenly when she saw the skunk. I was grateful when she complied with my stern order to retreat. Skunky also got the message. As she turned to leave the yard, she jumped over our cat, Sibalin, who was not the least fazed as she observed Skunky depart with amused scrutiny.

Skunks are regarded as power animals. Their message is respect. It is a valuable lesson we can all learn in this turbulent world. We generally love it when the neighborhood skunks appear, sans possible encounters with our two dogs, of course. We feel privileged to be included in nature's dance, for it reminds us to respect all beings residing in the Field.

SWEET MESSENGERS

Have you ever sat quietly, perhaps meditating, when a hummingbird appears next to you?

One evening, while meditating, a bejeweled hummer suddenly materialized by my left ear, hovering for a moment before zooming off into dusk's path to darkness. She often appeared in the following weeks, clicking away as she lingered beside me in my meditative reverie. She immediately inspired a sort of wonder, then inner silence within me.

I always feel blessed by hummers' appearances and marvel at their stillness and ability to change directions in a nanosecond—a good lesson for us all. We mortals engage in tasks that ensure our survival: working, eating, and sleeping. Humans tend to blaze through their days without tuning in to the world around them. A hummingbird sighting always reminds me to stop and be still, even momentarily.

We are a manifestation in a unified field that includes all living and organic frequencies. Realizing this assists me in tuning into the place where communication with all living beings becomes possible. As we become more attuned to this possibility, we can better attract real connection with nature and…harmonize with its beautiful dance.

THE LITTLE SQUIRREL WHO TRUSTED THE GIANT

One day, while walking through the living room, my eye caught a rapid movement flash along a far wall. I knew it couldn't be one of the cats as its movement was furtive. I quietly crept over to sneak a peek behind the couch. Even before I got into position, the creature dashed to the opposite side of the room. I hoped that it wasn't a giant rat!

I opened the front door, hoping to facilitate its escape from our house. Instead, it maneuvered quickly beyond the open door, disappearing around the corner and into my office to cower behind the bookcase. I made a noise on one side of the bookshelf; it darted to the other corner, finding its possible hiding place under a wooden cabinet.

Fortunately, the cabinet had a five-inch clearance at its base, so I lowered myself to the floor to peer underneath. In the corner was a baby squirrel, trembling in fear as it gazed back at me. No doubt: this was one of the offspring of our two tree squirrels that graced the property. My heart melted, and I knew I needed to rescue it before our cats got wind of this visitor.

I left the room to get a wicker laundry basket, then turned it on its side, nudging the open end to the front of the cabinet. I realized I would have to entice the squirrel into the basket, whose depth was about three feet as it lay on its side.

I took an even, deep breath and then projected one thought repeatedly to my small friend. "Go there, you want to go there," I repeated. I tracked a path from this cornered critter to the basket's opening with my eyes several times.

It took just a minute, and then a miracle happened. The little one took three tentative steps and then glanced my way. "That's right; you want to go there," as my eyes shifted toward the basket. Three more quick steps, then a look at me. Just three more, and suddenly, the baby was in the basket. I jumped up to lift the basket upright when the utterly unexpected happened - my squirrel friend leaped out of the basket and raced back into its corner.

My chances of getting a repeat performance seemed next to nil. I had to try. I conjured a new strategy. I would quickly place a towel over the basket's opening once the baby squirrel found its way back in. I would then gently right the basket and take it outside to free the temporary captive.

I dropped to the floor again, hoping the trembling baby in the corner would once more participate in her rescue.

"Okay, let's try again. You need to go into the basket. That's right; it's best if you go into that basket so I can take you outside. Time to be in your tree."

I then projected, "You are safe," and "I want you to be back in the tree."

My other projection was that it was a privilege for me to interact with it so intimately. It seemed to hear my thoughts; its gaze shifted from me for a long moment, then straight ahead into the looming abyss of the laundry basket.

Once again, it took three tentative steps, looking at me and then looking ahead. Then something interesting happened. It chose to be brave. It paused, then walked calmly into the back of the basket. I lowered the towel over the opening to enclose it for its journey outside to its natural habitat.

Before proceeding downstairs, I took a quick peek at this adorable creature, marveling at its trust in its rescuer. I carefully transported the basket to the property's edge and gingerly turned it on its side. In a split second, my little friend leaped out of the basket, over the wall, and into the welcoming bushes. With a rustle and quiver of a tree branch, it was gone.

This small rescue effort uplifted my heart and soul, reminding me of the privilege of connecting to nature through the Field.

SYNCHRONICITY: BATS IN THREES

Living in the city, I always welcome sightings of non-domestic animals. Over the years, I have observed that wild animals sometimes appear in my environment in groups of two or three. I now realize that some lesson or challenge is afoot when encountering the same animal in three different settings. When this happens, I quickly research the underlying meaning of this spirit animal to understand the learning opportunity I'm being offered.

One evening, I was drawn to something flying erratically around the living room. It took me a moment to realize it was a small black bat. Not a common experience in our household; I jumped into action as it appeared frantic in its search for a way out of the room. It jaggedly flitted its way through the ceiling's cross beams. My attempts to direct it out the front door were futile.

It needed a bigger opening. I strode over to the French doors and tugged them both open. I stationed myself alongside them, calmly pointing the way out with the sweep of my arm and the thought, "This way out." It only took a few moments before the bat found its way through the opening to freedom.

Just twelve hours later, another bat needed my assistance. This time, it was trapped within the tennis court where I was playing! It could not find its way up and over the chain-link fencing because it couldn't read the fencing obstacle with its sonar. After two runs around the inside of the court, it landed on the chain-link fence, panting. As it struggled to escape the enclosure, I realized I had to interrupt the match to study and possibly assist the fenced creature. It was mousey brown and shuttering with fear. I murmured to it, hoping to calm it and encourage it to aim higher in its flight.

Further attempts to escape were futile. I knew I had to go one step further. I gently nudged the bat to climb onto my tennis racquet so that I could escort it outside the court. With my gentle prod, it inched its way to the center of the strings. I slowly moved away from the fencing and thrust my racquet upward. It took flight and gained the altitude needed to clear the chain-link fence. Freedom!

A bit later that afternoon, I logged a third bat sighting, noting that messages from Spirit often happen in threes. While I was happy to assist my local wildlife, I now needed to know the meaning behind these three appearances of bats.

I got out my power animal deck to tap into a possible message from the Field. As always, I appreciated its insightful offering. Bats represent rebirth, initiation, extra-sensory hearing, and letting go of the old self, habit, or life groove. Relevant to me at that moment, I thanked the Universe for the message.

6

INTERACTIONS WITH THE DANGEROUS ONES

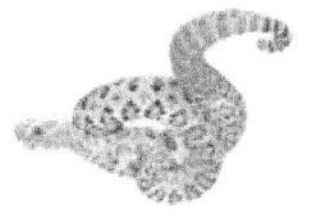

RESPECTING REPTILES

In addition to lizards, I also appreciate and respect snakes and the occasional iguana, which we enjoy on our trips to Mexico. I even held a baby alligator once in Ixtapa. I quietly stroked its head and spine, praying it would not be subjected to too many more months of being a tourist attraction. I hoped its "owner" respected its innate wildness and would soon set it free.

Even as a kid, I wanted to hold snakes, always fascinated by the beautiful patterning on their backs. I never wanted a snake as a pet, as I thought they should live freely in their habitat. However, I am not shy about getting close to our local non-poisonous snakes, especially if they require assistance. I am happy to encourage them to move off a busy paved road by sharing encouraging words. I usually stand some distance away at first and talk softly to them. I then encourage them to move to an off-the-road destination with the gentle motion of a stick. Yet there are times when I attune to their presence and nudge them out of danger with my thoughts and quiet encouraging words. Some people even accuse me of speaking Parseltongue from Harry Potter lore.

Only 10-15% of all snakes worldwide are dangerous. They are essential for keeping rodent populations in check. When hiking in their territory, be careful where you step and always keep your distance out of respect and for your safety.

RATTLERS HEAR MY THOUGHTS

In the late spring in California, one must be on the lookout for rattlesnakes as the weather warms, primarily on mountain roads. These native reptiles, waking from hibernation, glide out from their dens and take to the open trail to thaw themselves in the morning sun.

One unseasonably warm morning in mid-April, I was hiking with my dogs, Rune and Gracie, on one of my favorite trails in Santa Barbara. We came around a blind curve only to discover a nice-sized rattler sprawled across the road. I quickly brought the dogs to a halt behind me and commanded that they sit and stay. The dogs caught my tone, sat, and did not move a muscle.

My next thought was to get the snake off the road. I was concerned for its safety as much as the pooches because many uninformed people believe the best rattler is a dead one.

The dogs and I stood perfectly still, about 10 feet from the sunning creature. I paused to reflect on the best action. I wondered if I rolled a pebble toward the snake, would it slither off the road, into the brush, and out of harm's way? I picked up a small stone and rolled it toward the reptile. The snake immediately went into a defensive coil and issued a warning rattle. "Well, that didn't work." I centered myself with a deep, calming breath. Then I thought, 'Talk to it."

Without moving a muscle, I projected a clear picture to the snake that it needed to get off the road to be safe. I spied a sizeable, not-yet-blooming purple sage plant on the right side of the road, just a short distance from the rattler. "Unwind and go to the bush right there," I said softly. I visualized the snake uncoiling and slinking over to the bush. "You need to go to that bush," I repeated this direction several times as I pointed to the awaiting hideaway with my extended arm. I maintained a still presence.

A moment later, the snake uncoiled and side-winded its way off the pavement and directly into the undergrowth of the sage plant. After a moment, I snuck a careful look; the snake had disappeared. I said aloud, "Good job!" The dogs and I proceeded on our morning hike. I was thrilled that I had been in the presence of a rattler and that it seemed to register my directive for its wellbeing. Nonetheless, the next day, I doubted I had anything to do with the snake's march to safety.

A month later, however, I was in the back hills of Ojai, celebrating with my women pals at a beautiful retreat center. We decided to take a quiet morning hike into the backcountry in groups of two or three. I had gone ahead of the rest of the group.

I was an hour into our scattered hike when I heard panicked screaming. I immediately sprinted back on the trail only to find several friends had encountered a coiled rattlesnake, rattling its tail and viewing these ladies with a suspicious glare. I sprang into action, thinking that this was a "double-double" from Spirit. A double-double is when something manifests two times in a row as confirmation, should you doubt what happened the first time.

I gestured for the women to take a wide girth around the snake. They rushed into a clearing to the right of the path. I paused, took a deep breath, and approached the snake cautiously and respectfully, maintaining an appropriate distance of ten feet. The frightened women were calling after me to run. I motioned for them to be calm. I turned my attention to the rattler and, with a quiet mind, relayed that I wanted it to be safe. I spied a newly flowering shrub by the left side of the path that seemed like a good hiding place.

"You need to get to that bush," I offered repeatedly, sending the image of the snake migrating to the waiting bush.

Within moments, the snake uncoiled and made the short journey to the base of the mountain shrub, then disappeared. I slid over to its new haunt to check. It was nowhere in sight and safe from human intervention for now. A discreet smile disclosed my joy from aiding a fellow being on the planet. I motioned to my friends that the trail was now safe for use.

The more we respect all life forms, the more harmony and balance we will experience. While I would never go looking for snakes in the wild, I always do my best to safeguard my loved ones and, at the same time, preserve and protect my co-inhabitants on this beautiful earth whenever possible. I continue talking to all snakes, encouraging them to move off roads where they might get injured. And yes, they still listen.

BEARS, BEARS, BEARS

For a city girl, I certainly have had my share of bear encounters in this life. For some reason, I have never been afraid of them. I respect their presence in their habitat, noting that these creatures' behavior is highly food-motivated. Camping in California--especially in Yosemite or Sequoia--almost guarantees seeing a bear roaming through your campsite. I always found bear sightings exciting and have often had to hold myself back from running after them to say hello.

My first close encounter happened while backpacking in Yosemite in my early twenties on a late August backpacking trip with two of my besties and one of their new boyfriends. The days were toasty and touched by a warm late summer light. The evenings were quite chilly, warranting the need for down sleeping bags.

We had made the six-hour trek up many a switchback to a Tuolumne Meadows campsite on the upper end of Yosemite. The hike included a moderately challenging mountain terrain through pine forests that offered an authentic alpine feeling. We were headed for an area that offered a meandering stream that could provide a soothing footbath after a long day of trekking.

Tired after a long day on the trail, we pitched our tents and set up camp in an area with a natural kitchen made of boulders. Because bears were infamous visitors in the backcountry, I was trained as a young backpacker to hang any packed-in food over a high, extended branch and tie it off on the tree trunk. Before we got snuggled into our down bags for the night, I took all our food, put it in our sleeping bag knapsack, and hung it from the branch of a large tree close to our tent. "That will keep our food safe from the bears," I proclaimed knowingly to my tent mate.

The following morning, around 5 a.m., I awakened to a resounding thump. My tent-mate, also roused, grabbed my arm, then whispered, "What was that?" I cautiously looked out our tent flap to see a large bear up on a rock about 20 feet away, enjoying the repast from the downed knapsack. I gasped, "A bear just got our food. Shoot. Well, I guess we'll be fishing out of the stream if we want to eat."

Well, my friend was not about to have her food consumed by a bear without a fight, as she emphatically enjoyed her mealtimes. We locked gazes, then simultaneously drew four fingers into our mouths to produce our best screeching whistles. The bear paused in its gluttonous activity and glanced our way. We took one more courageous breath, then blasted the morning air with one more long shriek. Irritated at our carrying-on, the bear rumbled off into the surrounding forest. I quickly exited the tent and climbed onto the rock to gather our remaining food. The bag was shredded and now useless. Meanwhile, the ruckus had awoken our friends in the other tent, who stuck their heads out in time to see the bear take off.

Now quite awake, we all decided to get up and make breakfast. The rock where the bear had taken our food was just above the outdoor kitchen. The smell of coffee and oatmeal permeated the crisp morning air. The conversation was lively due to our pre-dawn visitation.

Our crew was just about to dig into our morning meal when Mrs. Bear appeared out of nowhere, taking a dominating stance atop her rock. Her indignant expression clearly said it all: "WHERE. IS. MY. GRUB!" Once again, we resorted to loud whistles and banging spoons onto our metal cups. The bear looked at us, confused that we dared to refuse her request to surrender the grub. She turned and lumbered off, never to return that day.

Within hours, other campers and backpackers filtered by our campsite, noting they were going home because they had lost all their food to bears. While we nodded in sympathy, we realized we now had access to the better campsites alongside a burbling stream. We pulled up stakes and headed up the trail for a better site.

This time, I learned my lesson. I tied the rope onto the remaining knapsacks with our food and threw it over the hearty branch of a ponderosa pine. The rope's other end was secured to the trunk of a sister tree ten feet away. In addition, I tied our billy cans (large coffee cans with hanger wire handles) to the rucksack and placed assorted rocks in them. If we heard the rocks banging in the cans in the middle of the night, we would know our chow was again under siege.

Sure enough, we awoke to a rhythmic clanging sound at the crack of dawn the following day. Our co-hikers called out to us from their tent to stop making the racket. There was a pause; then we realized we were all still in our tents. Alarmed, we stuck our heads out to see two baby bears in the ponderosa, swatting capriciously at our food sack.

With no hesitation, we began our siege of whistling and pot-banging. The baby bears, fortunately foraging sans their mamma bear, looked at each other for a split second, then trundled down the tree, scrambling off to the safety of their mother. We did not encounter any other bears for our remaining time in the backcountry. Perhaps the word was out that the grub was not worth the din those darn "two-leggeds" were making.

I have had various encounters with bears that, thankfully, have always turned out for the best. I have been known to call out to baby bears visiting the blueberry patch at our lake cottage, hoping to have a quick conversation with them. They always know best to run to their mamma bear.

BEING MAMMA BEAR

Over the years, I realized that 'bear medicine' represented the principle of Mother or mamma bear. I did not bear children, as my life's work seemed to be caring for my many patients. As time passed, our house served as a temporary home for different lovely women at significant passages in their lives. The first one, whose mother was my best friend, came to live with us during a family time of transition. Within the first few weeks, she came up with her name for me, "Mamma Bear" or just "MB." To this day, this is what she calls me.

The second woman lived with us while she completed her MFT degree. She became a much-loved house sitter to our four beloved pets, who considered her their big sister. She also called me MB. Upon hearing the moniker MB, the third 'adoptee' chose to call me Mamma Bear, introducing me as her mamma bear. Because of their residencies with us, I cultivated the art of nurturing the younger set. I now feel the power of bear inside me when it comes to protecting loved ones and those who are vulnerable.

WHEN YOUR POWER ANIMAL IS A COUGAR

Some of us have more than one power animal.

One of my most treasured power animals is the cougar or the mountain lion. I discovered this in an enigmatic shamanic journey decades ago. At the start of the journey, activated by the beat of a Native American buffalo skin drum, I had posed a question about my life's direction. I knew I had to experience a meditative journey to obtain the answers I sought.

The steady beat of the drum immediately plunged me deep into my long-ignored psyche. Once there, I was confronted by flashes of the challenges swirling around in my life. My breath quickened as I dropped into tracking these stresses, one after the other. Feeling overwhelmed, I wrestled with how I would resolve all the challenges confronting me in my life. Yet, I surrendered to going deeper within to find the answers.

Suddenly, a cougar profile flashed before me; its alert ears pitched forward in readiness. Just as I registered what I was seeing before me, its visage faded from my view. I pondered the meaning of its appearance to the continuing beat of the drum. Soon thereafter, another expression of the giant cat shifted into focus. This time, I found myself clinging to the neck of this cougar as it lunged forward, its pure power surging up through my body. I experienced empowered aliveness. The drumbeat pulled me even deeper into my subconscious. Where was this all going?

Then came the final vision. This time, the image of the mountain lion faced me head-on, staring intensely into my entranced psyche. Something exploded in me, perhaps a long-suppressed innate sense of power. I wanted to roar. I did, in the depth of my being. It was long overdue.

Now, as a spirit cougar, I was ready to stalk life's challenges and even be empowered by them. These presenting challenges and lessons would be my teacher. I promised myself that I would learn from them. As the journey wound down, I intuitively surmised that I had to use this inner cougar energy wisely, channeling it to empower others on their life's path of awakening.

This inner knowledge has never faded from my consciousness and continues to define my life path as a healer. I am always grateful for the opportunity to empower my patients and friends on their healing journeys. But what does it mean to have a mountain lion as a power animal?

Mountain lions represent agility, wealth, and beauty. In addition, they act as fierce protectors through life's lessons. More than anything, they represent the power to act or pivot at a moment's notice. They are noted for their strength and ability to stalk their prey with determination and silence.

Cougars or panthers are native to California and occasionally show themselves to humans. More than ever, bears, bobcats, cougars, and coyotes are making their way into our neighborhoods, as their habitats have been encroached upon, and climate change has affected food and water sources. Although they can threaten humans and their pets, these felines are essential to the balance of nature. They and their habitat must be protected for our world to survive.

The following story illustrates the possibility of living in harmony with the more dangerous part of Nature.

WHEN DEATH STALKS YOU

Years ago, a friend shared his experience of encountering a big cat in the backcountry of Santa Barbara. After several hours of hiking up one of our local trails, he stopped to perch atop a boulder outcropping jutting out from the hillside. While resting there, he decided to meditate. Soon, he was enjoying a deep meditative state. But then something changed - he distinctly felt a presence behind him.

While remaining calm, he opened his eyes and slowly turned his head to glance behind him. Out of his peripheral vision, he spied a mountain lion crouched twenty feet above him. The cougar's eyes were trained on him. Remaining in his state of meditation, he took a slow breath and paused, appraising an appropriate course of action.

He immediately realized that if the cougar was going to attack him, he had no path of escape. With that in mind, he slowly turned his head forward and returned to his meditation, aware of the possibility of meeting his demise. You could say at that moment that Death was stalking him. Yet, as each moment passed, nothing happened.

Finally, after what felt like an eternity, he slowly turned his body again to look over his left shoulder, keeping his breath even and calm. To his surprise, the cougar was gone.

When he told me this story, my only emotion was a blush of envy. I so wanted to be that close to a mountain lion, in meditation, and live to tell the tale. The only thing that could have been better was if the mountain lion had nudged me for a pet!

Be careful what you wish for, though…or wait and see what the Universe has in store for you!

I MEET MY POWER ANIMAL

On one bright and sunny Memorial Day weekend, my partner and I drove up to a local mountain trail with our two dogs. We planned to ride our mountain bikes up a winding road with Rune and Gracie. Rune, a blonde lab mix, was 11 or 12, while Gracie, a large reddish Shepard-Setter, was about nine. We packed a lunch and set off for Figueroa Mountain, a summit anchored in the San Rafael mountains, north of Santa Barbara. I wanted to video the ride down with the two dogs in tow. However, this was before GoPro and iPhone video, and I was going to handhold my video camera.

After an arduous yet invigorating mountain bike trek up the road, we stopped at its crest to enjoy our picnic. We kept our eyes on the dogs so they wouldn't wander off. Rune acted strangely that day, pacing back and forth on the road with alert glances tracking the ridge above us.

After we finished our meal, I noticed that Rune appeared as if he was not feeling well. Because of this observation, I decided not to film the slow journey downhill, as he was dragging his feet. Yet, despite his apparent lethargy, both dogs surged ahead of us. I kept a keen eye on them, even as they rounded a curve just ahead.

Forty yards away, I noticed both dogs pulled up short. Rune went into an attack stance posture. I did not want him getting into a dog fight, so I barked, "No, Rune, No!"

I peddled into high gear and caught up with the dogs in moments, my trail mate just behind me. As I pulled up close to the dogs, I surveyed the object of their immobilizing attention: a mountain lion. Crouched just 15 feet away to my left, this female mountain lion's long, slender tail swished in apparent anticipation of an eminent meal. Her prey, the two dogs, were positioned on the other side of me near the road's ledge, frozen in place.

My Mamma Bear instincts sparked into action. Without thinking, I threw my bike down with a clatter and plunged toward the cougar as she sprang toward my canine children. I didn't consider the danger of my protective impulse.

The next few moments felt as if time slowed waaaayyy down. My body seemed to flit through the air as my arms lifted above my head, fingers curled like a pouncing tiger. My face contorted into a grimace as I screamed, "Noooo!" The cougar, mid-leap, glanced in my direction. She diverted from me at the last fraction of a second, just three feet beyond the dogs. As she sailed by them and into the nearby gnarled bramble, their heads slowly tracked her powerfully muscled movement as if she were an inanimate object casually passing them.

The cougar leaped over the roadside gravely berm and into the thickest, thorny thicket I could imagine. Strangely, there was nary a crackle of a sound as she vanished from sight. Without a thought, I rushed to where she had entered the silvery green density. I could not discern where she had entered the bramble as there was no notable break in the bush.

The dogs were still bound to their spot on the dirt road as if nothing dramatic had happened. My partner had witnessed the cougar's near take-down of our dogs and was duly alarmed for our safety, even though the cat had vanished into the brush.

At that moment, I experienced a strange composure, almost an exhilaration. My fingertips groped my pulse point to confirm my perception of calm. I half wondered if that cougar had been some form of spirit manifestation due to the dog's calm reaction to a dangerous potential attack. Without my biking mate as a witness, I would have logged my experience as a strange hallucination.

The fact that we all had a brush with death did not enter my mind for a second. Instead, I was thrilled to the bones that, for those elongated moments, I was this close to a mountain lion.

Even though I sensed the mountain lion was gone for good, it seemed time to leave.

My riding partner quickly offered to pedal down to fetch the car and bring it back up the road. Rune was still not himself. I gathered the dogs around me to begin our slow descent downhill. We paused for a moment to listen for any sound of a stalking cougar but were offered only the precious silence of the mountain. We collectively maneuvered down the winding road as an elated smile spread ear-to-ear. That cat was beautiful. My heart pounded with joy. She was a force of nature as she crouched, muscles taut, tail a-swish. I felt her power surge through me as I slowly descended the mountain with the dogs, happy I had time to be with this once-in-a-lifetime experience. And grateful that no harm came to any of us.

The essence of the miraculous hung about me in the days that followed. For me, it was indeed a gift from my power animal, the cougar. I inwardly thanked her spirit for not taking my dogs--or us--to the 'other side'!

THE HAWK AND THE SNAKE

Not all power animals are dangerous. Many are benign and may appear in our lives in various ways.

One day, many years ago, I was talking to a new friend who had recently moved from Mendocino County. She had moved there as a teenager, lived on her own, and had been a vital part of that community. After living there for many years, she realized it was time to create a fresh start for herself.

She packed her car the morning of the move, her heart weighted with sadness. Was she making the right decision? She was leaving so many friends.

As she pulled out of town to head south, a flash of tawny red drew up from the highway's center divider, passing right in front of her windshield. This flash of wing and tail signaled her that it was a red-tailed hawk. It had a writhing snake in its clenched claws. As it crossed her vision path, she sensed that this was a powerful omen validating her decision to leave the community she had for so long called home.

Her story sent shivers down my spine. I contemplated and marveled at her tale after we hung up. It struck me that the Universe often gives us powerful signs about our unfolding path on this earth. It's up to us to pay attention.

The next day, I met with a group of new friends to bike ride in the wine country of Santa Barbara. I was training for the Santa Barbara triathlon, which included a 52-mile ride through hilly backcountry roads. This ride seemed like the perfect challenge.

As we made our way through the back roads of Santa Ynez, a very steep hill appeared ahead of our pack of riders, curving around to the right at its peak. After a brief assessment, I decided to attack the upcoming hill as a training maneuver. I got up out of the seat and powered up the hill as fast as possible, leaving the others behind.

As I banked around the top of the curve, a blaze of red struck up from the median line. I had startled a red-tailed hawk with my sudden appearance. In its talons was a writhing garter snake. As the hawk spiraled skyward, it flashed me a piercing glance, then dropped its prey back onto the road ten feet from me.

My gaze tracked the upward flight of the hawk as I threw down my bike to rush to the stunned snake's side. Puncture wounds were evident where the hawk's claws had pierced the snake's skin. It was still alive. I did not want a car to run over it. I moved my bike off the road and foraged for a strong branch. Once located, I carefully strung the snake over the stick for transport to the side of the road. I gingerly set it down under a bush, hoping it might recover over the next few days. I silently wished it well, then turned to retrieve my bike, happy I had rescued the snake before the other riders had converged upon it.

The remainder of the pack of cyclists rounded the curve, halting when they saw my downed bike. After I satisfied their curiosity about my intervention in the hawk's meal, we jumped back on our bikes to continue our trek down the back side of the hill. I felt sad to leave the snake in its injured condition, yet I realized that humans could only intercede so much in Nature's dance.

As we departed, I reflected on how my new friend had relayed her similar experience of the hawk and the snake the day before. Her story enhanced the relevance of my interaction with these two beings. Reflecting on my friend's tale, I realized that this was a sign that she and I would be lifelong friends, which is true to this day. I could not wait to return to Santa Barbara and share with her how these two animals graced my ride with their interplay in the circle of life. Once we connected, we mused on the possible meanings behind our mutual sightings.

To this day, I value the appearance of red-tail hawks as a significant omen for me, as it is considered a primary messenger from Spirit. Its cry often offers me a message of support when I most need it. I love watching them ride the flow of the thermals, spiraling ever upward to observe the world below.

7

TALES OF THE RED-TAILED HAWK

INITIATION INTO THE POWER OF THE RED-TAIL

Many years ago, I spoke with a friend on the phone who was well-attuned to nature. During our conversation, he heard a distinctive shriek in the background. "A red-tailed hawk is flying over your house right now," he informed me. Something clicked inside, and I instantly knew that this bird was special to me. From then on, my eyes began searching the skies for the familiar float and swoop of the red-tail.

Sometime later, this powerful bird began appearing in my meditations to assist me in problem-solving life's ongoing issues. The messages were subtle but directive. Moreover, they gave me confidence that I had a guardian spirit keeping an eye on me. They also appeared in various shamanic journeys.

During one such journey, it appeared suddenly in my mind's eye, looking over its left shoulder with a piercing glance that said, "Follow me into the unknown." Follow, I did, on several occasions, and each time, hidden truths were revealed to me about what was unfolding in my life.

In Santa Barbara, we have our share of turkey vultures, which can be mistaken for hawks. However, you can always distinguish the turkey vulture by its tottering skim over the backcountry as it searches for carrion. Red-tails, however, elegantly catch the updrafts and appear to hold their position in the sky with no effort.

The red-tailed hawk can fly very high, even to the point of disappearing. We witnessed this while gathered on a hilltop with pyramidal mountain peaks as our backdrop. On one New Year's Day, we offered beautifully decorated life arrows with our prayerful intention for the forthcoming year.

On this occasion, just moments after we had finished planting our arrows, one of the ranch owners spotted a red-tail hawk navigating through the bottom of the canyon below. We all paused and reverently watched its elegant rise via the subtle thermals. It slowly drafted upwards, riding the deep canyon breezes upward, pausing momentarily at our eye level, circling there several times. It then spiraled skyward until it became a faint dot against the gorgeous azure sky. It finally disappeared into the welcoming arms of Spirit with our humble New Year's intentions.

During one challenging year, I saw or heard a red-tail hawk daily, no matter where I was in our bustling city. Their piercing cry always jutted into my heart, reminding me to remain connected to the divine, no matter what challenges unfolded in my life.

Red-shouldered and red-tailed hawks grace various Santa Barbara locales. On one local hillside, a beautiful copse of tall and majestic eucalyptus trees offers the perfect nesting areas each spring for a resident pair of red tails. They produce two hatchlings yearly that spend their first weeks screeching for food.

I sense that I can communicate with this family of hawks. I introduce myself annually to the teenage hawks learning the ropes of flying and hunting. If I spot them at a distance, I quiet my mind and invite them to enjoy a circling flyover to show them off to friends and family. They usually oblige me, as you will see in the following tales.

HAWKS HEAR THOUGHTS

One spring day, while on the tennis court, I spotted one of the young hawks gracefully maneuvering the airspace above me. While gazing skyward, I mentally invited this youngster to circle over me in a flyover. I repeated my request several times in my mind, with proper respect, of course. "Would you be so kind as to circle overhead to let me know you can hear me?" and, "I would so love it if you would fly over me this so I can see how beautiful you are up close." To my surprise, the teenage hawk ignored my humble entreaty. However, I did not take offense and figured it might take time for the newly airborne to understand my vibrational invitation. Well, I was right. It did take time - exactly 24 hours.

The next day, I was back on the court when one of the teenagers seemingly tuned in to the previous day's appeal. It floated gracefully over to where I was playing, then circled multiple times, just twenty feet above me. On its eighth loop, my new avian friend glanced downward, our eyes connecting for a split second. With a tilt of its head, it seemed to ask, "Will that do?" My nod said it all, and away it flapped to join its sibling in a nearby grove. A quiet exuberance powered me through the rest of the game.

A few days later, while walking our two dogs on a mountain road, we spotted three red tails tumbling over each other in apparent play. Two of them were smaller, possibly the hawklings from the week before. Perhaps the mother of the two landed on the arms of a telephone pole just ahead of us. I instantly felt an opening in my heart, primed for connecting with this gorgeous mamma hawk.

I extolled its beauty out loud. Mrs. Hawk glanced down at me, then, with a flash of wing, flew away. Within moments, it was barely a speck in the sky. A bit disappointed, I closed my eyes and quietly asked her," Please come back and circle above me to let me know you can hear my thoughts."

My gaze then turned to the young hawks as they dove and jabbed at each other in a playful skirmish. I marveled at the nature of youth across all species. Suddenly, the older one appeared out of nowhere and circled directly over me for three large passes. Joyful, I expressed my thanks and blessed it with heartfelt gratitude. Once again, aglow with this special connection to nature, I felt at one with the Universe.

The Third Visit

You are an omen to me
Alighting in the winter tree
Sharp look, then flight again,
Until the next day
You shriek in your fly-by
A flash of burnt umber.

Over the oak
I search the skies
For the third visitation
Truly auspicious, you
Find my mother's house
On her birthday
And shred your caught meal while we watch and
Aspire to your beauty and intensity.

8

BLESSINGS FROM THE BIRD TRIBES

AVIANS AS GUIDEPOSTS

Birds, as power animals or totems, have a special place in the lore of unfolding spiritual paths. Ken Carey wrote Return of the Bird Tribes, which speaks to the presence of our aviary friends on earth, inspiring us to connect to the loftier aspects of the spiritual side of life. Reading Carey's book caused me to pay attention to the myriad avian lifeforms that grace our world and meditate on their deeper spiritual meaning. Once I began watching the skies, I began noticing beautiful synchronicities occur between their appearances and events that unfolding in my life. I began to treasure the gift of all forms of birds that appeared locally and when being in more exotic habitats.

As you peruse the following list of birds' resonances, can you relate with any of these avian friends and their spirit message? Do any appear often in your life? What do you feel when you encounter them? Has their presence ever signaled a need to pay attention to what is unfolding on your life's path? Have you enjoyed a sweet or intriguing encounter with one of the bird tribes? Do any of these feathered ones appear in your dreams?

When you peruse this list, do any messages sing to your heart?

1. Crow - Supreme Order of the Universe
2. Robin - Voice of Love
3. Swan - Marriage of the Polarities
4. Raven - Depth Magic
5. Wren - Birth into Consciousness
6. Seagull - Knowledge of Enlightenment
7. Dove - Inner Peace
8. Blackbird - Wisdom to Surrender
9. Eagle - Return to Spirit
10. Owl - Death to Ego
11. Sparrow - Innocence
12. Cockatiel - Vibrational Resonance
13. Toucan - Trickster Wisdom
14. Gala - Freedom to Fly
15. Hummingbird - Touch of Caring
16. Mockingbird - Call to Self-Knowing
17. Blue Toucan - Soul Knowledge
18. Condor - Connection with the All
19. Vulture - Materiality
20. Goose - Freedom to Express the Self
21. Hawk – Direct Communication with Spirit
22. Larks - Direct Contact with The Mother
23. Ducks - Resonance with Emotional Fields
24. Bluebird - Memory of Ancient Wisdom
25. Peacock - Hidden Beauty
26. Falcon – Connection to the Mystical
27. Ibis – Intelligent Factoring
28. Canadian Goose – Synchrony with the All
29. Loon – Grace of Heart Connection
30. Pelican – Expression as Oneness
31. Cormorant – Power to be Free

THE BABY BLUE JAY SAYS, "THANK YOU"

Blue jays are, by nature, scrappy, sassy, and always opportunistic regarding treats. My brother has trained one to sit on his shoulder or foot while he enjoys his morning coffee. This jay even hopped her way into his house to observe him during his quiet moments of yoga and meditation.

I love this story a friend shared with me. She marveled at a young jay's expression of gratitude despite the mother jay's admonitions.

"I awoke with Gaia in my heart this morning, the sun beaming through the trees, the quiet morning interrupted by the laughing call of woodpeckers. I was thinking about a small female blue jay who had mysteriously locked herself in our crawlspace. As we opened the door, it defiantly called out and scared us with a flap of her somewhat formed wings. Her fluffy head cocked as she looked at us, wondering what to do, then flapped wildly into the deeper reaches of the crawlspace.

We opened the doors, but the baby jay did not fly out immediately, unsure for her safety. We went and got her water and bread and left her to her own timing. About an hour later, we saw her drop onto our deck. She scuffed about, then noticed her admirers in the window, viewing her with rapt attention. She hopped straight toward us, cocking her head, and blinking sweetly at her delighted rescuers. Overhead, her mother squawked wildly to protect her. As we watched her antics, we realized she wanted to say "thank you" for letting her out of jail. She calmly sat there for a bit; we shared this precious moment, eye-to-eye. Finally, she flew off for her feeding and flying lessons from her mom and dad jay. I was lucky enough to see her the next day, scratching for bugs under the trees with her scruffy black head."

21 CANADIAN GEESE

One late summer afternoon, while staying at the East Coast cottage, our next-door neighbor and I decided to engage in our traditional swim to the end of the lake. As soon as we dove into the refreshing waters, we noticed the lake's end was populated by a line of Canada geese. Having never been around these birds, I was excited to swim over to gander a good look at them. As we approached, I noticed these beautiful birds were scouting for bits of morsels on the shoreline.

My swim pal became engaged in conversation with someone who was sitting on the beach not far from the geese. While treading water, I counted the number of geese nibbling their way along the shoreline: there were 21 in all. I soon determined who appeared to be the head of the flock by its alert attention to my presence.

I allowed myself to drift in towards one goose, which had a distinct presence about it. This goose focused its keen attention on my approach. I slowly drifted towards it, keeping only my head above the surface so I would not appear too big to the head goose.

As this goose was tracking me with its attentive gaze, I tuned into it with my presence. With respect, I repeatedly offered this thought to its Field, "Would you be so kind as to please come in the water and swim with me?" As I projected this into the Field, the goose threw an alert glance in my direction, then back to his pack, then back to me.

Within moments, it decided to honor my request. It waddled towards me, then silently glided into the lake. Immediately, each goose jumped up from their sand digging and followed their leader into the lake. Before I knew it, all 21 geese were swimming in a line parallel to the shore, with me in tow. I kept a respectful distance of 15 feet while they streamed along the lakeshore. The leader would look ahead, then over to me, to ensure it was safe for the flock and, perhaps, that I was tracking with them.

The three to four minutes of our slow paddle were heavenly; I felt at one with the flock. I knew it would be short-lived, though, as we were at the narrow end of the lake. Moments later, the lead goose turned toward the shoreline, and all twenty geese followed in formation. I maintained my distance in the water and offered a subtle yet happy nod to the flock as they immediately went about their business of foraging.

I turned and swam back to our dock, so grateful that, once again, nature had provided me a connection to feeling one with the

Field. I then remembered that Canadian geese connect us with universal synchrony.

CONFIRMATION OF THE FIELD

Years later, a second opportunity to swim with my migratory friends presented itself. It was my last night at the cottage for the summer. There had been enough rainy days that I had not swam down to the end of the lake with her or by myself. I was missing my swim companion of prior years as well. It was a muggy evening, and a plunge off the end of the dock sounded inviting. I dove in, feeling the layers of the warmer top water and the cooler lower water register as delicious refreshments.

As I came up for air, my neighbor's sing-song call floated out from her cottage, "Valerie...do you want to swim?" It had been two years since we had engaged in our chatty breast stroking to the end of the lake, so I answered, "Of course! Get your suit on and get out here! I've got to hurry as I have rice on the stove." Soon, she was gingerly wading into the lake's waters before diving in to join me.

As we stroked and chattered about lake issues, I noticed Canadian Geese at the end of the lake. Although my swim pal was not thrilled at their presence for the waste they produced in the lake, I was excited. "Maybe they will come in and swim with me again?" She did not think so, as they were now up a grassy hill, pecking for bugs and worms to feed their new families. There appeared to be two sets of mammas and papas with six teenagers in tow. Nonetheless, I remained hopeful and began my silent entreaty for this flock to come and swim with me.

It had been six years since my last swim with their kind. Would they recognize me? Would there be a notation in their morphogenic field, "Uh, the bobbing head with the wet blond feathering is okay. It likes us." I hoped so, as it had been so rainy during my stay that year that I had not experienced many interactions with the lake's wildlife. I was missing my crew of lake beings and our sweet interactions.

As I swam closer to the shore, I called out to them, "Come swim with me!" They ignored my request, nibbling away, their long necks extended towards the slope dotted with wild grasses and tiny flowers. I called again, this time calming my mind and breathing evenly. I was now close to the shore.

Suddenly, they looked up from their picking, pivoted toward the lake, and waddled down to the beach. They entered the water seamlessly and began paddling toward me. I immediately turned to swim alongside them. The head gander lined up next to me, and the flock dutifully followed. We were swimming in tandem! Again! I was thrilled and kept an even pace with this year's flock leader. We glided along the shore as the day's end sunrays flitted over their elegant feathering, tucked into their svelte bodies. Sublime timelessness ensued.

I then spied a new addition to the lake this year: an extended aluminum dock blocking our usual swim path. Because of their height in the water, I knew they could not make it under the structure. I mentally asked the head goose if they wanted to divert around the dock or turn back. The leader sized up the barrier, glanced at me, then maneuvered a seamless 180 turn in a split second. The entire flock mimicked this maneuver in one synchronized movement. They were undoubtedly attuned to each other in the Field.

I swam back with them for a few more strokes, then thanked them as they exited the lake for more foraging. I also gave thanks to the lake for gifting me this opportunity to align with its inhabitants and confirm that I was a joyful and willing participant in its field, once again.

Maybe those Canadians will come looking for me next time. And yes, I did burn the rice.

THE WHITE OWL OF CHANGE

In the shamanic worldview, the appearance of owls may herald an imminent death. Because of this, there is an underlying fear when they make their presence known by hoo-hooting in the dark of night. Not so with me. Although owls did appear outside my window to portend my two grandmothers', I appreciated their message.

The appearance of an owl may also signal an evolutionary shift needed on one's spiritual path. Always ready to take the next step, I feel honored to witness their hoots to one another. I make sure to pause and contemplate what lies in store for me.

My first experience with an owl occurred during my third year of college while attending UC Santa Barbara. I practiced transcendental meditation daily yet sensed that I needed a different format of connecting to my spiritual nature. I also knew I needed assistance in discovering this new spiritual path.

One afternoon, while meditating in my room, awash with a warming sunlight, a desire to align with a spiritual and service-oriented group arose from my depths. I sat quietly with this thought and intuited that I wanted a teacher rather than a guru. I also needed a spiritual practice that assisted me in evolving both as a person and a healer.

While in that deep state, I humbly asked Universal Oneness to lead me to the perfect spiritual group most supportive of my soul's purpose during this lifetime.

Two days later, while driving along a darkened frontage road in the late hours of the night, a large white owl with an extensive wingspan suddenly appeared out of nowhere. Now illuminated by my headlights, it beat its enormous wings oh-so-slowly, sashaying from one side of the road to the other, ensuring I fully registered its mysterious appearance.

A mile or so down the road, it spun off to the left and disappeared into the dark of the night. Instantly, I intuited the owl's appearance as a positive omen for my recent prayerfully offered intention.

Once home, I excitedly shared my excitement over seeing a white owl in Santa Barbara with my roommates. I was met with blank stares.

In less than a week, I received a promising phone call. A young man asked if he could introduce me to his meditation practice before leaving UCSB. I was incredulous and questioned him on how he found me. He stated he had gotten my phone number from his mother, a woman I did not know. The only detail he offered was that he was willing to come to my house and teach me a process to connect to my soul. I immediately invited him for the following Saturday.

When the doorbell rang, I opened the door to discover a diminutive, studious-looking young man with thin, wispy hair. He seemed so much younger than me – this surprised me. I invited him in, and after an exchange of formalities, we settled in to talk about the technique and his meditation group.

He shared that he had learned this technique from two meditation teachers who led a group of like-minded practitioners meeting weekly in Los Angeles every Friday night. As he explained the initial exercises of the practice, my soul instantly resonated with its power. I could feel its effect immediately as calming and centering.

The group's focus filled my requirements for a spiritual practice: a teacher rather than a guru, a simple process for enhancing my path of awakening, and the aim to be of world service. Not only did I embrace the practice daily, but after six weeks, I was invited to meet the meditation teachers at their hillside home in Los Angeles. I drove down with my new friend on a Friday night and met with one of the teachers in his book-lined study. He observed as I successfully employed the initiating technique, then invited me to join the group.

I faithfully participated in the planetary healing work for the next eleven years, rarely missing a Friday night. The offerings and practices provided essential healing tools to clear my emotional and energetic blocks. The teachings imbued me with critical spiritual principles that have influenced my life thus far. Most importantly, both teachers impressed upon me the importance of working for the good of all beings.

I am eternally grateful for their offerings and the white owl's appearance on that darkened night, sashaying its way down that road to illuminate my forthcoming spiritual path. Its appearance at that moment in my life will always remain a delicious mystery.

I eventually discovered that white owls are not indigenous to Santa Barbara.

THE OWL APPEARS TO CONFIRM

Three years later, while attending one of the meditations, I nervously announced to the group that I planned to enroll in chiropractic school to get my degree. Everyone, including the teachers, offered a murmur of encouraging congratulations. We then settled in for a blissful evening of meditation.

The meeting ended, and as I got up to leave, the same young man offered to join me on the way out. We made our way to the cars, parked on a steep hill overlooking Griffith Park. Once there, we paused and silently surveyed the city lights below. After a moment, he turned to me and said, "You know, Valerie, for a while now, I have had this vision of you as a doctor. However, I always see you with an old-fashioned doctor's bag, like in the olden days."

As if to punctuate his intuitive assessment of my future career, a great horned owl suddenly appeared in a stately yet slender cypress tree barely five feet away on an exposed branch. We froze, barely glancing at each other in disbelief that such a beautiful creature was so close to us.

The owl fixed its attention on us with an unblinking stare. Moments passed, then - it intently turned its gaze to me. Decisively, it winked at me with one eye. I took a sharp breath in. Then, as additional punctuation, it burst from the cypress with one swift leap. We turned to follow its path of abrupt departure, watching it wind down the curving road to disappear into the dark of the night.

"Well, I guess that says it all," was the only thing my friend could say. I was speechless.

Little did I know then that for the next forty years, I would treat thousands of patients and lead that many meditations. This signpost from the avian world would be one of many that would guide the trajectory of my life toward the art of healing and teaching others to heal.

Years later, I wrote the song "White Owl of Change" as a homage to these sublime and mysterious creatures.

My White Owl Of Change

I wonder why I have seen you
My White Owl of Change
Appeared you did within my dreaming mind
A thousand words of wisdom in a wink of an eye
Bidding me fly
Bidding me fly
Bidding me fly

Before my path, I've oft times seen you fly
I'm seeing the power you hold
You bid me fly to my inner sky
A place of feel and flow
Total letting go
To my Self

Oh, wise one, you bid me seek it
Though I stop, for fear of falling
I light not long, for your distant calling
Bids me fly, once again,
My White Owl of Change

The road appears so long
I can't see the end
Yet I feel you strong within me
As you soar, into the light
I'm winging so high
Into life's flight
My White Owl of Change

9

THE CALL OF THE LOON

Over the years, I have spent significant time at the 100-year-old cottage in New Hampshire. On my first visit there, my partner and I arrived in total darkness and were relegated to camp on the floor of a screened-in porch. The lights were out as we quietly tucked into our sleeping bags for the night. After a long day of travel, I fell asleep instantly.

In the middle of the night, a strange, distant, mournful cry echoed through my consciousness. I bolted up, alert. Could it be a wolf or coyote, romantically howling at the moon? I was excited to hear them so close! I listened intently for more of that haunting cry, then lay back down to fall into a peaceful slumber.

At dawn's first light, I sat up to gaze out the porch windows into lush, wooded surroundings. I was shocked to realize the lake was a mere twenty feet away. The barn red cottage was perched on a small hill at the east end of the lake. From there, its Y shape stretched westward. The shoreline was rimmed with tall pines, reaching toward blue-gray mountain peaks that hosted a notable notch in its ridge line. I later discovered that notch would be responsible for channeling strong winds that whipped up sudden squalls that directly targeted our end of the lake.

That first morning, upon awakening, I informed my partner that wolves roamed the lakeside at night. She quickly dismissed this fantasy. "That was a loon," she clarified, shaking her head. A what? Being a West Coast girl, 'loon' was the root of looney! She then explained that they were a large, black and white waterfowl, much beloved by the residents of the Lakes Region of New Hampshire.

With that mystery solved, we climbed into camp clothes, out the front door, and clambered down a rooted path to the dock. Behind the aged wooden dock was a weathered red canoe, complete with carved wooden seats, paddles, and seat cushions. What could be better? We maneuvered our craft into the still morning waters and began our explorations of shore and open waters.

Over the next week--and then years--the lake became my friend: a gracious hostess providing me with a myriad of extraordinary nature experiences that would become treasured memories. Sightings of mink, bear, fox, bald eagle, wild turkey, dragonflies, perch, owl, ducks, flying squirrels, rabbit, porcupine, coyote, and Canadian geese became a source of inspiration, offering a profound feeling of connection to the natural world. These lakeside inhabitants also became my inadvertent teachers about the nature of the Field. In this way, they nurtured my life as a healer of humans.

Beyond a shadow of a doubt, my very favorite beings on the lake are loons. They are almost mystical in their ability to suddenly appear, silently glide across the lake, and then magically disappear with nary a ripple on the azure lake surface. During the summer, loons sport a beautiful variegation of white on their black feathering. Fiery, ruby eyes accentuate their noble profile. Their call to one another cuts right into my heart like a knife, often rendering me teary.

The loon's cry has several distinct sounds, including its mournful howl, which echoes and resounds across the lake. Another sound is a thrill of a trill that warbles through one's soul. I always wait for the first loon call of summer. Somehow, I am not fully initiated back into lake life until I hear their hauntingly beautiful cry.

In late spring, loons return to their adopted lake from the Eastern seaboard, where they winter. Lakes freeze over; oceans do not. These beautiful birds lose their variegated summer markings to a dull, thicker winter coat when they migrate to the eastern coastline.

Loons mate for life, and the pairs hopefully produce two chicks yearly. Our beautiful small lake is usually home to one nesting pair. Lake residents do their best to protect the loon's chicks from several different predators, with the bald eagle being a particular threat. They even provide them with a nesting basket located just offshore. We look for the loon pair on our sunset motors around the lake as they gently float on the flow of lake swells with the hatchlings secured on their backs.

LOON LOVE

The first time a loon passed close to our dock, I wanted to dive in and swim with it. Loons, however, are typically elusive, steering clear of humans. Before I could gather my wits to jump in, the loon had vanished with a graceful arc of movement into the depths. Although this repeatedly happened during my first visitations to the lake, I was never discouraged, knowing my desire to connect with this intriguing waterfowl would manifest one day.

Finally, after many years of annual visits, my patience was rewarded. One bright, cloudless morning, I sat on our dock with only the sounds of local twittering birds as company. I fell deep into meditation, feeling very expansive in my heart. Then something nudged me to half open one eye. Before me, not ten feet away, floated the vision of a loon. I immediately opened the other eye but stayed in my meditative reverie. The loon bobbed on the lake's ripples, maintaining its position at the end of our dock.

Instinctively and with meditative reverence, I expanded my energy field to include my floating visitor. In response, it immediately glanced at me with one succinct motion. We locked eyes in what felt like a blessed eternity until it resumed the surveyance of its surroundings with quick movements of its head.

After a few moments, I decided to test my connection to the loon via the Field. I silently projected, "If you can hear my thoughts, make a small sound." A moment passed; the loon looked at me, then let forth a discreet warble. I froze, not quite believing what I had heard. I needed confirmation. "Okay, to let me know that you can really hear me, could you make that sound again?" Again, a pause. Then, the loon lifted its head and issued a second warble. My heart burst with a flush of joy. The loon could hear me!

Soon, the loon drifted away, turning its attention to the middle of the lake. I padded down to the end of the dock and quietly slipped into the water. The loon seemed to wait for me at a human-appropriate distance. I slowly swam toward it; surprisingly, it did not move away from me. We floated together for a while. Then, the loon stopped paddling and turned to look back at me. I paused. Appearing to feel safe, it tucked its head under its wing as if to take a snooze. I patiently treaded water until the loon lifted its gaze back to me. We then resumed our swim, at peace in each other's presence. Then, perhaps because it was feeding time, my new lake friend took a deep dive, only to appear on the other side of the lake just moments later.

After that, 'my' loon would often appear, floating in place, in front of the cottage. Friends would kid me, saying, "Your boyfriend is here waiting for you." I would jump into my bathing suit and fly down the steps to our small sandy beach. As I entered the water, I would speak in a cajoling voice, imagining it could understand my thoughts and feelings. I am sure the neighbors thought I was looney! Although it sometimes took the whole visit to manifest our avian-human connection, I always procured my loon swim each summer, counting it as the highlight of my summer sojourn.

MY LOON POSES FOR A SONG

Several summers later, this same loon found his way to the cove in front of the cottage one lazy July day. I was happily lounging on the dock when I spied it on the other side of our moored blue and white runabout. As an experiment, I started singing a particular ditty that I sing to connect to animals in the wild. It drifted closer to the boat, seemingly intrigued by my playful tune. My spirited song drifted upward to the cottage, and my friend, curious about its continuing repetition, came down the winding path to investigate.

I caught her questioning look but did not stop singing as the loon had now come quite close to the dock, apparently hypnotized by my engaging chant. I dramatically motioned with my hands for her to "please fetch my 35mm camera from the cottage". She spotted the loon, nodded recognition of the unfolding situation, then bolted up the path to nab it.

I realized the loon might follow me if I carefully picked my way along the rocky, poison ivy lined shore to our sandy beach a hundred feet away. The camera was delivered within moments, and without a second thought, I began my treacherous journey, sidestepping the poison oak.

I finally stepped down onto the sandy beach and gracefully slipped into the warm lake water, still warbling to my entranced friend. The loon floated even closer to me until it was just five feet away. Still singing, I began snapping photos as the loon struck different poses while fixing its ruby-eyed gaze on me. Completely elated by its trust in me, I experienced an indescribable connection with this handsome fowl. I snapped several perfect, iconic shots of my avian friend while continuing to serenade him.

Our interaction occurred over a quarter of an hour, with me crooning through the entire episode. But even a loon has its limit. After nailing his photo shoot, he shot me an upward side-glance: "Are we good here?" I nodded my satisfaction. He swiveled 180 degrees and paddled away, presumably for his next exciting adventure--or at least an afternoon snack.

In the following years, the loon seemed to know when I would arrive at the cottage by showing up a day or so before, stationed calmly in our cove. While I never had such a close encounter with him again, I was often graced with his sudden appearance during the day and his lonesome calls at night.

Sadly, we learned of the loon's demise years later. He had swallowed a fishing lure with a hook. Although a concerned lake dweller rescued him, the veterinarian could not save him through surgery. Tears still gather in my eyes when I think of that unnecessary loss. It remains a somber reminder of the preciousness of life and that we must consider ourselves stewards of the Earth's natural wonders or face their extinction due to our careless actions.

THE LOON CONNECTION RETURNS

After my loon friend passed on, I lamented that I experienced no real connection with his successors as they were not making their usual appearances at our end of the lake.

During one of my stays at the cottage, time was running out to experience my loon connection of the year. I pondered what I needed to do to remedy this situation.

The next day, I was drawn to sit lakeside at the edge of the dock. I gingerly walked the steep, root-bound path. Once seated, legs dangling into the water, I closed my eyes and mindfully opened my heart to my surroundings. I so wanted to connect to a loon, any loon. After a few quiet moments, I posed this query to any loon able to hear me, "Where is my loon connection? I miss connecting."

Immediately, I heard this answer, "You have been too busy to tune in." Oh, right. I had been spending more time with neighbors and less with nature. So, I asked to connect now and got the message to open my heart and be still. I did. I then asked, "Where are loons on the consciousness spectrum?" The answer I received did not surprise me as much as it made me put my head in my hands and weep.

> "Loons are more conscious than most humans as they do not consciously destroy their habitat."

All I could do at that moment was sob uncontrollably, my tears falling into the lake. At that moment, I vowed always to do my best to preserve this precious planet.

My tears subsided, my gaze gradually shifting to the other side of the lake. There, I beheld a loon paddling through the usual midafternoon wind swell. I silently asked the loon if it could come closer. Immediately, it changed course and began to drift toward our property. This moved me even more, causing more tears to flow.

Moments later, I was reminded of an impending appointment by my partner. Knowing I had only a few minutes to spare, I called out to the loon to please come closer. Under it dove, soon surfacing at the water's edge of our property. Excited, I headed for the stairs leading down to the sandy beach. Halfway down the stairs, I saw the loon surface before me, just a few feet offshore. It paused for a timeless moment, looking pointedly in my direction, then turned and executed a perfect arced dive under.

My heart again swelled in appreciation for realizing my dream of a loon connection in the intimate setting of this beautiful lake. It required that I quietly submit my request to the Field and be grateful for another small miracle.

At dusk the following evening, I roosted at the water's edge, thinking about climate change and the planet. I asked for the guidance I needed to assist me in making a real difference here during my short time on Earth. A flash of movement suddenly caught my attention. A bald eagle burst from a grove of trees just to my right. It swooped down towards the lake, glimmering in the early offerings of sunset, circled back toward me, then sublimely lifted away, adroitly landing upon a distant treetop.

Its appearance lifted my spirits. As a power animal, they symbolize a connection to the Oneness. Of course! I took this as a direct sign from Spirit to remain connected to my inner guidance as well as my intention to do good for all beings! The word 'trust' then drifted up from my subconscious. Oh, I had to trust that Spirit would guide my journey here. Right. I closed my eyes, then surrendered to this simple notion, grateful for my time at the lake and the lessons it always provides my heart and soul.

WHEN LOONS ARE HEALERS

The steward of the lovely cottage shared this heartwarming tale of three loons that gathered around her to offer solace at a time of profound grief.

"I sat beside my elderly mother on hard, plastic, adjoining seats in the New Hampshire Department of Motor Vehicles. It was a typical muggy July afternoon. Mom and I were waiting for my 89-year-old father to renew his license. My mother, my lifelong best friend, had suffered memory loss for the last decade but always knew who I was.

Unexpectantly, she turned to me and asked me my name. Thinking she was joking, I playfully stated that my name was "Fred." She accepted my false answer without hesitation and then asked where I lived. A feeling of terror crept over me. I instantly knew she was sincere and did not know who I was.

"Mom, I am your only daughter … are you all right?" I could see a glimmer of confusion flash through her eyes. "I don't have any daughters," she said reluctantly.

I asked her more questions, hoping this was a fluke. My heart pounded as the din of the DMV faded from my awareness. I felt scared and uncertain. I then realized that she did not recognize me as her daughter. At lunch, just an hour before, she had known who I was; now, I was a stranger in the seat next to her. Without warning, a switch had flipped. Alarmed, I grappled with the feeling that I had lost her, perhaps for good.

During the car ride back to our house, Mom still did not recognize me. My father and I were highly distraught by this sudden shift in her memory, although we had been warned that this might happen when she was diagnosed with dementia a few years earlier.

We returned to our cottage in the late afternoon. Without pause, I bolted down the path to the lake and pulled the faded red canoe into the water. I set my sight on the middle of the lake, motored by the grief gripping my heart. When I could paddle no further, I flung down the oar, taken over by uncontrollable sobbing. I had lost the one person in my life who had been my anchor through thick and thin. Suddenly, she was gone, no longer my parent. I choked on my tears, sputtering, as I wailed into the rising dusk of the lake.

Then I heard it – a cooing sound. I looked up from my tear-streaked hands to see three loons surrounding my canoe, uttering a soft, warbling sound. For twenty minutes, this family of beautiful birds circled me, emitting sounds tinged with the miraculous.

Despite their common shyness with humans, these loons made the journey across the lake to comfort me during one of my life's most devastating events. Their soulful cries as they slowly paddled around my boat offered me the comfort I needed during my descent into despair. I didn't want to leave the comfort of these blessed creatures. I couldn't bear the thought of returning to the house and confirming that my mother no longer recognized me as her daughter.

As dusk's soft light faded, I reluctantly canoed back to the dock, moored my faithful transport, and tearfully walked up the wooded path to the house. During that brief traverse up the path to the softly lit cottage, I realized I had to summon a brave front for my parents, especially my mother.

Over the next few years, I learned to accept that our relationship had moved on to a different phase. While my mom remained loving and sweet with me, it was now my turn to mother and care for her.

I never heard the loons offer those comforting sounds again."

Animals of all types find ways to offer solace to other beings they usually avoid. Hearing this tale reminded me of the power of comforting those needing love and support.

LOONS BID ME ADIEU

On one of my last days at the cottage, we pushed out onto the lake, nestled in our kayaks, to explore the surrounding well-wooded shores and coves. Soft, filtered sunlight streamed over the edge of the surrounding forest. Of course, we were not-so-secretly hoping for one more loon sighting. It was the impetus behind our quiet paddling out.

It did not take long for a sighting. My co-paddler spotted the sought-after loons, starboard off our kayaks. The pair floated at a comfortable distance from us, bobbing in concert with the lake's gentle rhythm. We eased off our paddling motion, observing them with appreciation and genuine awe. My partner prodded me to energetically connect with them. I expanded a peaceful field around us, including our avian friends in my projection.

Quiet, blissful moments passed when the pair suddenly turned 90°, paddling straight toward me with apparent determination. The head loon, presumably male, led the procession. The pair were ten feet away from me in moments, very close for human contact. As I was low in the water, the leading loon and I were almost eye-to-eye as he pointedly approached me. As he paddled toward me, he would snap his gaze down the lake and then back to me, repeating this motion several times. Now, five feet away, we locked eyes. I could feel that he was directing a communication to me. I received it in a wordless flash, yet with no immediate translation.

I suddenly realized that this fowl sensed I wanted to connect with them to bid my adieu for the year. The meaning of that held gaze was suddenly clear to me in a flash: "We showed up. Are you good?" My wide grin said it all.

With one final glance, the beautiful pair, with their black and white dappled plumes, diverted their course and gracefully sashayed around the front of my kayak. Seconds later, they took an arced dive, the lead loon and then his mate disappearing forever from our sight.

"It was your field; your field attracted them," pronounced my friend, who had observed the whole unfolding of this magical interaction.

As if their manifestation on this glorious morning was not enough of a gift to us, a beautiful white feather floated over to me with just a hint of black variegation on its tip. I gracefully scooped it up and gazed at it with gratitude for this precious interlude with my avian comrades.

Later, I wondered aloud if my first loon, who had graced my company often over a decade prior, had left a footnote in the 'loon morphogenic field': "This one is okay; she reads our energy." I remembered a similar look tossed my way after our extended interlude on our shore. That night, I was graced with a welcomed deep slumber, so deep that I did not hear their refrains of farewell in the wee hours, which were recounted to me by my partner the following day.

These many encounters with loons and other avian friends have redirected my life's intent toward opening my consciousness to the possibility of the miraculous. To do this, I must find my inner silence. It's not always easy in this dense, chattering world.

As I recount still another miraculous tale of interacting with the lake's field, a prayer now comes to me:

> May I quiet my inner thoughts so I may attune to Nature - our most immediate bridge to the beautiful under-light of our world. May all humans be humbled by Nature's offerings and be gracious in their interactions with all that provides the beauty of our earth. May I be inspired to be present in the presence of the luminous field of light within me and all things so that I may remain connected to the Divine Presence, which I now know is just a blink away.

10

DOCKSIDE FRIENDS

THE LAST FISH I EVER CAUGHT

When I was young, my father used to take my brother and me fishing off a pier in Oceanside, California. We would set up our chairs and gear and sit patiently for hours, hoping to catch a fish, which often did not happen. I did not care, as being with my dad on a warm summer beach day was always a joy.

It had been years since I had thrown a line into a lake or the ocean. Then, one warm afternoon, while dockside on the lake, I was inspired to pick up a vintage fishing pole leaning against the dock's resident pine tree. I looked out toward the lake's center, then intently cast a line out. I loved flinging a rod, listening to the burrrr of the line going out and the smack of the lure hitting the water.

After casting out, I sat down, hand loosely gripping the cork handle as I chatted with friends and relatives perched on the dock's weathered bench. Halfway through our conversation, I stole a glance lakeward and noticed my bobber had disappeared. I raised the rod to check the tension on the line and felt a tug in response. I had a fish! Excited, I strode to the end of the dock and pulled and reeled as the fish flopped about on the lake's blue sheen. It only took a few minutes to get it dockside.

I grabbed the fishline and reached for the end of the line to admire my catch. Then I saw it: the hook jabbed through the mouth of the fish. The next thing I knew, I was sobbing, ashamed and heartbroken. Why these feelings now?

This was a moment of reckoning I did not anticipate. I did not need to catch and kill this fish; I had plenty of food. It certainly was not a sport I wanted to engage in any longer.

Blinking through my tears, I carefully unhooked the fish and knelt to gently escort it back into its watery home. It sashayed away, no doubt relieved to regain its freedom. I took a deep breath, swearing I would never fish again. Then I shuffled back to my friends, who were perhaps baffled by my sudden tears.

Moments later, that fish looped back, coming in so close to where I was standing on the dock. It flashed its silvery tail out of the water, creating a notable plop. In that split moment, I was convinced that spunky bass tossed an upward glance my way as a 'thank you' as it pulled off its splashy maneuver.

As the bass darted off, my eyes welled up again. That fleeting flash of connection with that fish soothed my heart and blessed me with this veracity: even fish are conscious. I realized there is always the possibility of a bridge between any being and the human who can relinquish their attitude of superiority to experience it.

While visiting the cottage now, I chase fishermen away from our little cove as I feel very protective of those aquatic beings who grace our neck of the lake.

THE LOVELY MRS. PERCH

During my first visits to the lake, I noticed a yellow perch just below our aged wooden dock, rippling inside the "V" of two rocks anchored in the shallows. I immediately dubbed her Mrs. Perch. Just eight inches of sass, she sported a big black spot on both sides of her body.

Mrs. Perch would flit about her territory, always returning to a defensive position, ready to take on any threat to her post. I assumed she was waiting for bugs and ants to fall from the tree limbs that hung over the dock that would become her next meal. I would even go to the trouble of collecting the errant ant that appeared in the kitchen, traipsing down to the dock to feed Mrs. Perch a tasty morsel.

Over time, I decided to have an underwater interaction with Mrs. Perch. I donned my goggles and bobbed on the lake's surface until I hovered over her territory. She tolerated me since I kept my distance. Perhaps she realized that I had provided snacks for her.

One day, I maneuvered down to her level. She rose to greet me, wiggling up to my mask to survey this giant creature. I wondered if she saw herself in the reflection of my goggles. I put my finger out to see if she would interact with it. At first, she prodded it with her open mouth. But then I committed the obvious, egregious human error: I reached out and gently touched her black spot. Shocked by this intrusion, she darted beneath the dock and vanished. For good. I berated myself for being selfish with my curiosity.

She must have told her aquatic mates about the colossal monster infiltrating her territory, for not only did she not return for many years, but no one else assumed her post.

More recently, I wandered down to the dock one early sunlit morning. The lake was pure glass with nary a ripple across its expanse. A golden green glow gilded the tumbled rocks lining the lake floor. I was enjoying the lake's serenity when my gaze dropped to the sandy opening between the conjoining boulders below.

A new Mrs. Perch had arrived! She appeared younger than her predecessor, petite, but just as bossy. She tolerated my appearance looming above her. As penitence for my prior misdeeds, I collected some ants and tossed them to her. But this time, I knew to keep a respectful distance.

I will no doubt continue to hunt for treats for whoever maintains the "Mrs. Perch" post, especially if those black ants do not know enough to stay out of the kitchen.

SMALL MIRACLES ON THE LAKE

When I am attuned to the lake, small miracles occur regularly. One such provider of these offerings is the flitting and flirting of iridescent dragonflies.

Some evenings, while I am enjoying my five o'clock swim, dragonflies buzz me, taunting me to race them down to lake's-end. I delight in their dance as they buzz the lake surface with athletic prowess, zipping and zagging with their vibrant expressions of life. What's not to love about their colorations: iridescent blue, pink, gold, and so many variations of exquisite vibrance. They skim the lake's surface, daring to sometimes mate right in front of me. Occasionally, they land on the top of my head, the tip of my nose, or even my third eye! I imagine they survey me as a bobbing island to explore or even hitch a ride on as they zoom by.

On one overcast afternoon, we paddled out on the lake in the canoe for the afternoon jaunt. A hefty black and yellow striped dragonfly landed on my hand as we began a lazy row to the cove of white lotus buds, located just around the bend. Because I was the designated paddler, I quickly transferred our hitchhiker to my knee for a more stable perch. I told the dragonfly we were headed to one of its hotspots.

Appearing content, the winged creature remained on my knee as I paddled through the quiet waters. We included it in our conversation as if it could understand our every word.

Soon, we were deeply embedded in the center of a patch of blooming lotuses, ablaze with the buzz of various airborne insects. Once the dragonfly realized the bounty of nectar ensconced in the landscape, it jumped ship, soon zigzagging its way through the fragrant wonderland. We soaked in the serenity afforded us by our slow-moving canoe journey while observing our fellow traveler jag about.

This may have been its secret destination all along, for it did not ask for a ride back.

Ahhh, to connect with an insect! No creature is too great or small to enjoy an afternoon delight, experiencing another tail of the miraculous.

REQUEST: FULFILLED

One year, my repeated requests made aloud to my dragonfly friends to land on me as I skimmed the shoreline went unfulfilled. I had also yet to experience my desired share of animal interactions. Perhaps it was due to a busy social schedule or more rainy days than usual. I was feeling a vague sense of loss. By my final day there, I mused that Nature and its Field were ignoring me.

But Nature has its own rhythm, which, most times, I graciously accept and acquiesce to. Through experience, I have learned to offer my requests and patiently await a response. Relinquishing attachment to specific outcomes sometimes manifests the most curious results.

On that last day, a twist of fate designed that I would offer a yoga class on our wooden dock, with the lake and her counterparts as a backdrop. I commenced the Saturday morning session with students privy to my previous yoga classes on the deck. We were all excited to be together again with the beautiful Lake Kanasatka.

Twenty minutes of warm-ups, and we were now ready for standing poses. Warrior I, II, and pyramid pose were lined up to fortify our strength. As I assumed my Warrior I pose, a tiny tickle alighted on my index finger. My gaze turned to view its source; a dragonfly had landed on the web between my right thumb and index finger. It did not just alight, it anchored. Even as my hand swayed from one pose to another, it remained on its post, shimmering bronze for five minutes as I shifted through our standing postures. Of course, I took a few moments to share my visitor with those on Zoom.

With the mission for a landed visit fulfilled, my dragon-friend buzzed off, no doubt to satisfy other invitations made via the quantum. Not to be outdone by a mere dragonfly, the local bald eagle flapped by us moments later, acting as a messenger of completion for my time at the lake. This was the same bald eagle that deemed us worthy of landing on a low branch above our dock, hopefully disregarding Mrs. Perch as a possible meal. Nature has its balance, though, and we are but its privileged observers.

This dragonfly was not the only insect to respond to my vocalized requests for visitation. A sizeable dock spider took up residence a bit close to me at the corner of my mat, calmly observing my cobra pose as I utilized what I call 'spider fingers' to raise my upper body off the mat. Once we rose to practice our standing poses, it sprang from the dock into the water below.

I have always treated spiders with respect. I walk them outside via their single-spun thread or politely ask them to please bring down the mosquito population in exchange for us leaving their webbed homes in the kitchen intact. It seems to work out, with all of us tending to Nature's balance.

Other insects on the lake have responded to my requests for an appearance. Several nights before heading back to the West Coast one year, I complained that I had not witnessed any fireflies dancing in the blueberry bushes at dusk. A moment later, one blinker responded to my announcement and choreographed a light show to my satisfaction. The performance continued for my remaining nights, with several light dancers appearing to impress us as we slowly rocked our chairs into the night's tranquility. Why do their luminations always feel like a magical gift to us humble humans?

11

PLAYFUL FRIENDS OF THE SEA

You may remember from my initiation into the miraculous that it was my dolphin friends who taught me that all animals—of both land and the sea – have an intelligence beyond our comprehension. For many, just being near dolphins in the ocean is a healing experience. To hear their underwater sounds and calls thrills and assuages the soul into harmonious bliss. Innumerable stories of positive and intelligent interactions between humans and dolphins abound.

DOLPHINS AS HEALERS

I am not generally supportive of wild animals being held captive in zoos or marine centers unless they are injured and cannot survive in the wild. But there are situations where our friends in the wild consent to serve as a conscious bridge to humans in exchange for food and connection.

Many years ago, a friend invited me to a weekend workshop to swim with dolphins. It was hosted by a behavioral psychologist who focused her research on autistic kids. She was utilizing dolphin interactions to encourage these children towards increased socialization. The proceeds from our workshop would help fund her research sessions with the younger set.

On a muggy Florida June day, my friend and I joined six other participants at the dolphin center tucked into an inlet off the Western coast of Key Largo. We gathered on a dock to get the lowdown on how the center's trainers worked with their charges. They assured us that the dolphins were not captives and could venture out of their enclosures into the open seas. The fish dinners were too enticing, so the half dozen residents mulled around, waiting for their next fresh meal. Each dolphin had a name and a personal underwater pen to call their own.

The workshop attendees were offered six interactive sessions in the water with these powerful beings of the sea. The trainers outlined their requests and regulations to guide our interactions with the dolphins for their safety. After these instructions, buckets of mid-morning snacks were brought out and tossed to expectant mouths.

Once fed, the bottlenose dolphins reacted with their unique personalities in playful abandonment. Their intelligence and ability to relate to their human caretakers and the day's visitors were immediately apparent. I could not wait to get in the water and get close to these beautiful and charming beings.

First, we were introduced to them individually as they bobbed with their wide-open grins in front of the excited group. They seemed just as happy to meet us as we were to swim with them.

Finally, we got the signal to jump in with masks and fins for our meet and greet. Elated, I dove into the pool with my best racing dive.

Upon command, one dolphin would swim up to an attendee and offer its dorsal fin to grab to transport them across the length of the holding pool. It was thrilling to experience their innate strength capable of quickly escorting each of us through their watery medium.

We then had swim time to cavort with them in their space. I was anxious to see if I could communicate with them nonverbally. I had already experienced their psychic powers in my sailing journey in Mexico, and— I wanted more!

Immediately, a female dolphin nosed her way up to my mask to peer into my eyes. As an experiment, I engaged with her in underwater conversation. I projected my hopeful invitation to connect with her, and she responded with burbly chatter as she bobbed at my mask. Totally a blast!

On day two, I entered the swim area and treaded water while awaiting our next directions from our facilitators. Bobbing up and down, I realized I felt out of sorts. I wasn't sure why. While pondering my inner state, I experienced a nudge to my backside. I turned to look behind me and discovered an older female dolphin had sidled up to me. She did not move on but remained dutifully by my side. Immediately, I sensed she was transmitting comfort and an insightful message that was not yet clear to me. As I floated with her for those few minutes, I could only hope to translate her transmission eventually.

Her nurturing presence soon uplifted me. I felt more positive and connected to myself. I marveled at her intuitive awareness and her inclination to be of service. When she sensed her mission was complete, she drifted away, inspiring me to continue my exploration of her world.

Soon afterward, a male dolphin swung over my way and graciously offered to swim with me. Grateful for the invitation, I reached for his back fin. He pulled me into the pool's depths, sunlight illuminating the bubbles streaming from his undulating body as he powered us downward. I held on for dear life, thrilled to be experiencing this spontaneous ride with him.

In my excitement with this new aquatic friend, I had forgotten to take the necessary deep breath to endure a long ride. I panicked but projected a mental SOS to my transporting underwater guide. He immediately pivoted, powered me up to the surface, and waited as I took a deep breath through my snorkel. He then escorted me back underwater for a proud tour of his watery environment.

Soon, he sensed I needed air again, bringing me back to the surface. Now relaxed, I inhaled deeply, and down we dove. After a few moments, the rascal headed to the underwater doorway to his pen. As we came up for air, everyone on deck was laughing. "He took you into his private boudoir!" the center owner chortled. News to me, this was usually off-limits to us wee mortals.

Down again, we went back out for another spin around the swim area, and after a few turns, he again attempted to get me alone in his enclosure. This time, I let go at the door, wanting to behave myself! As I surfaced, I heard peals of laughter from the peanut gallery. The dolphin bobbed up to the surface, looking at me with a questioning glance. "Hey buddy, you know I have to follow the rules!" Darn.

Although my jaunt with him was over, I knew I would always treasure my underwater excursion with him. I felt more in tune with myself as I hoisted myself out of the water with a big exhale. That's dolphin magic for you.

LEARNING HOW TO FLOW TOGETHER

Over the years, I wondered how dolphins performed their trick of synchronized swimming next to each other, as I had witnessed on my sailing adventure in Mexico. Finally, I got my answer the day after my time with the female dolphin.

As I awoke from a deep sleep the following day, the translation of her telepathic message to me was clarified: when dolphins engage in synchronized swimming, they link up sideways, heart-to-heart. This made perfect sense. I was so excited by this revelation that I asked my traveling pal to engage in an experiment with me. When I explained the premise, she was also intrigued. We reclined side-by-side on the motel's plush carpet and inhaled the humid Florida morning air, dropping into a deep meditative state. Focusing on our heart centers, we linked them sideways with an infinity flow pattern between us.

The effect was immediately energizing while we synchronized our attunement with each other. The process affected our overall energy for the rest of the trip, creating a lovely harmonic resonance with each other that continued well beyond the trip and to this day.

Perhaps our dolphin connection experiment was somehow responsible for the next mysterious event that unfolded the following day.

MORE DOLPHIN MAGIC

After an exciting last day of dolphin play, we decided to indulge in an early dinner. We chose a restaurant close to our hotel room and, as we entered, noticed it was devoid of other customers. We sat at a table by a window with a view of the harbor and bathed in the warm sunlight filtering through the tall masts of boats swaying with the incoming tide. After we briefly surveyed the menu, a waiter approached to take our order. We both selected iced tea and the salad bar. Our server turned and pointed to the door of the salad bar room, then left to bring us iced tea. My friend excused herself to visit the ladies' room; I headed straight for the door to the salad bar.

As I entered the room, I noticed two folding tables arranged atop a small platform at one end. I walked across the room and stepped onto the platform to inspect the offerings. It hosted a variety of vegetables, salad makings, and toppings arranged over trays of ice. As I stood gazing at the selections, my mind went blank, and time seemed to stop. I blinked several times as my attention came back to the room. I shook off the feeling of disconnect, then picked up a plate to create my perfect salad.

With my dinner in hand, I stepped down from the platform and returned to our table. As I approached, my friend stared at me with a suspicious look as I crossed the room with my salad in hand.

"Where have you been, and where did you get the salad?" She pointed to my plate, heaped with goodies.

I tossed my head toward the door where the waiter had directed us. "That door, where the waiter told us to go."

She looked even more suspicious now. "I went into that room looking for you. You were not there."

She added that she had seen me enter the room on her way to the ladies' room. When she was done, she peeked into that room, noted the salad bar, then wondered where I had gone. Did she have the correct room? Something felt off, so she returned to the table to wait for me. Now, here I was with my plate heaped high with a salad.

We stared at each other for a minute, then verbally attempted to create a scenario explaining the discrepancy in our perceptions. We ran the sequence of events several times with each other, then surrendered to what seemed impossible.

Had I disappeared?
Where had I gone?
Did I register what happened?
If I had disappeared, why?

We could only guess it had to do with our time with those enchanted beings of the sea. Perhaps swimming with them had changed our perception of time, or maybe I had disappeared for those brief moments.

We continued shaking our heads over this mystery for quite some time.

DOLPHIN RECEIVES A HEALING

A few years later, another friend and I visited the West Coast of Australia. We were equally crazy about dolphins, so we rented a car and drove 1,000 kilometers up the coast to Monkey Mia, a remote beach known for its friendly dolphin population. This beach had become so popular that it required a lifeguard to monitor human interactions with the resident dolphins. The pod was so interested in humans that they would come to shore to interact with anyone who showed up.

We were allowed to wade in the water but asked not to touch the dolphins. I immediately noticed one of them had skin issues on its dorsal surface. I inquired about the lesions, and the guard informed me that dolphins' skin often burns in sunny shallow waters. I asked if I could offer healing to the dolphin if I did not touch it. I was given the go-ahead with a wave of the lifeguard's hand.

I waded in several feet and approached the sunburnt dolphin. I mentally asked it if it wanted me to work on it. The dolphin floated over and stationed itself under my palms. I allowed neutral healing energy to flow from my hands to the damaged skin. The dolphin seemed to like it and stayed with me for several minutes. When I was done, it shimmied away.

Being a good swimmer, I decided to see what would happen if I stroked out to deeper waters. Happily, a half dozen dolphins tracked me beyond the breakers and cavorted under me, making several passes as I mentally called out to them for close contact. Their sonar sounds tickled my ears and my solar plexus. While these curious beings did not offer me a dorsal fin for a ride, I felt they were checking out this human who worked on healing one of their own.

DOLPHINS ARE PSYCHIC

Dolphins often abide by human telepathic requests for a timely appearance in the Santa Barbara coastal waters. I usually put forth my playful request for one of their swim-by appearances on my way to a beach day. Once I spot them up the coast, I run down the beach the opposite way to have time to swim out and experience their promenade along the shoreline.

Often while officiating a New Year's Eve ceremony of 'letting go of the old.' I put forth a mindful request for a visitation from them to enhance our sacred process. It is always a delight when they appear, especially when we are at the point of 'releasing the old' into our small bonfire. Their appearance usually elicits cheers from the participants.

One does not have to do a special ceremony to have dolphins respond to a request for a drive-by, as evidenced by this next story.

DRIVE-BY MANIFESTATION

One beautiful late spring eve, four friends and I gathered at a favorite restaurant perched on a grassy cliff overlooking the blue expanse of the Santa Barbara channel. It was high tide on a clear, unseasonably warm evening. The Channel Islands seemed to loom closer than usual, side-lit by the sun as it hung in the western sky through ambered clouds. Everyone at our table shared equal exuberance over being together again after the drudge of a chilly winter.

Once seated, we all ordered drinks and food, aware of the rising tide and the proximity of the breaking waves as they rolled in towards the cliff's rocks. The sun was just beginning its sunset dip onto the western horizon. The salt air was warm enough to enjoy the evening without a wrap.

As we settled in for an evening of lively conversation, I suggested that we collectively "request" the dolphins to do a swim-by in front of where we were seated. This prompted a resounding collective "Yes!".

"Let's call in the whales while we're at it!" added one friend.

"As long as we're putting our orders in, let's have them breach!" I furthered.

"And flip their tales at us," countered my friend.

We closed our eyes for a few blessed moments and focused on manifesting our intentions. With a nod of our heads, we opened our eyes and then clinked our glasses together in celebration of the evening ahead.

Our group immediately sprang into lively chatter as we caught up on each other's recent exploits. Suddenly, one friend noticed the rise and fall of dolphin fins, perhaps four. I jumped up from the table to sprint to the cliff's edge to observe their calm, rhythmic passage. My heart swelled once again, viewing these oceanic friends. Soon, having made their appearance directly in front of us, they disappeared into the ocean's depths. I returned to the table to settle in with my lovely friends.

It did not take long for our next wish to manifest. A woman at a table next to us pointed toward the cliff. "Look, there's a whale!" We turned to see the dark back expanse of a whale moving slowly through the rolling ocean, spouting its salty spray. The whale then breached a marked distance of six feet out of the water, directly in front of our table. As it did, it seemed, at that moment, its single eye looked right at me before slowly sinking into the rolling waves. Then, with a final flourish, the whale manifested our third intention with a swish and flash of her tail.

We clinked our glasses again, celebrating the beautiful beings who not only heard our humble requests but could manifest themselves so close to shore and in such a short arrival time. We were united in our gratitude that these tuned-in beings chose to make a swim-by appearance at our dinner gathering. How could we not feel blessed? Magic continued to hang in the air long after their swim-by!

A few minutes later, our server came to the table and commented that she had never witnessed a whale breaching in the six years she had worked there.

Humans have much to learn from cetaceans. They are intelligent, brave, playful, strong, and powerful and have rescued humans, dogs, and other species. Moreover, they are tuned in and responsive to those beings that respect and honor them as co-inhabitants of this beautiful planet. I always consider their appearances on our Santa Barbara coast a blessing. I hope humans will work to preserve their environment to secure their continued presence in our oceans.

12

BEASTS OF BURDEN

Over the years, I have been around people who own animals that they rent out for use by tourists. Some proprietors fail to treat their working animals with the care and respect they deserve. In some cultures, animals used for transportation, such as horses, donkeys, camels, and camels, are often overworked and abused. This will cause them to be unresponsive to commands, bad-tempered, or ill. I have found that if you give love to the animals who are helping you, love will be returned.

ANCIENT TRANSPORTATION

I will not hesitate to speak up if an animal is being abused. Such was the case when we traveled to Egypt and visited the Great Pyramid. We wanted to ride out into the desert to view the surrounding pyramids. We were presented with the choice of a camel or a horse to journey to a lookout where we could photograph all seven pyramids in perfect alignment.

As our group met with the men providing these animals, I saw a young man beating his camel. Immediately, I stepped up to the boy.

"How do you expect them to respect and obey you if you do not respect them?" I asked.

"Oh, but these camels are mean!" he replied.

I told them that Americans do not like to see animals abused, and if they wanted people to rent their camels, they needed to treat them better. To prove a point, I did not accept the reins presented to me but instead turned and offered a comforting hand towards the camel's neck, who reacted to my kind gesture with a subtle nod.

To further illustrate my displeasure, I migrated to a different concession and chose a horse to rent. My fellow riding pal followed suit, and soon, we were saddled up and heading out beyond the seven pyramids. Soon, we were galloping over wind-swept dunes, imagining ourselves in ancient Egypt, with head scarves flowing behind us. After a spirited ride to the hills overlooking Cairo, we snapped the perfect photo of all seven ancient structures from an ideal vantage point.

Later that day, we were escorted to the Bent Pyramid at Dashur. It was one of the earliest constructed pyramids. Unusual in shape, it stands alone in a barren desert expanse. A guide was standing duty with his camel, who sprawled out on the warm sand like a giant doggie. I asked if I could pet his lovely cohort. He nodded.

I respectfully approached the camel and reached out slowly with an open palm. He received my gentle touch on his head with aplomb.

Then, a group member noted that the camel lifted his face toward mine. "Why don't you kiss him?" he said with a laugh.

Never wanting to miss an opportunity to commune with a beautiful animal, I slowly lowered my face towards his muzzle, and we engaged in an almost kiss. Connecting with this lovely, gentle soul was a beautiful, once-in-a-lifetime moment. Happily, a picture was snapped, which I will always treasure.

PROFOUND PRESENCE

In many parts of the world, elephants are captured from the wild and sold into a beast-of-burden existence. While many people misuse these animals for the tourist trade, some sanctuaries purchase these abused elephants and offer them a comfortable home to live out their remaining lives.

Elephants are herd animals. In the wild, they can be fiercely protective of their own, with humans as their primary predators, slaughtering them for their tusks to be sold as ivory. Despite that, there are many stories of elephants' intuitive and intelligent interactions with the more compassionate members of humanity.

When Lawrence Anthony, an elephant rescuer, passed away from a heart attack, two herds walked in a funeral-like procession for half a day to come to this home to mourn his passing. How could they have known that he died? They stood in solemn vigil, stationed at his gate for two days. On the third day, they quietly departed and made the long journey back to their habitat.

Sadly, baby elephants are stolen from their mothers and herds in various countries, sold into a beast-of-burden existence, and exploited as a novelty in the tourist trade. These young elephants are then chained and forced to live on busy city streets, crying out because they are severely traumatized by being taken from their mothers. Fortunately, several animal activists have now established elephant sanctuaries. They purchase these abused elephants from their 'owners' and escort them to the preserve to live the remainder of their lives with their new herds.

We had the good fortune to visit one of these elephants preserves in the Mae Taeng District in Northern Thailand. Within the expanse of this sanctuary, elephants are not ridden. They are fed a healthy diet and are free to roam the property. They even produce young and interact with humans in a controlled manner.

We were offered the opportunity to meet one beautiful older female elephant named Mae Ping. Mae's quiet yet powerful presence emanated an ancient soulfulness as we gathered around her. One of her handlers shared her history and invited us to connect with her individually. I was thrilled at the opportunity, as I have always admired these very intelligent beings.

Whenever I am in the presence of an unfamiliar animal, I quietly extend an inviting palm toward them to measure how they respond. On this occasion, I slowly approached Mae with my extended hand; she responded with a nod of her wizened head. I took this as her invitation to connect.

As I gazed into one solemn eye, I was moved to tears as her countenance expressed her many years of trauma and oppression.

I then placed my hand ever-so-gently on her forehead and moved my head to the back of my hand to introduce myself and my intention to connect. Within moments, I could feel her enormous presence encompass me. With that, I could feel her physical pain from her advanced age and past treatment by humans. Yet, I also experienced a quiet acceptance of all she had endured in her long life.

I then emptied my mind and allowed healing energy to flow from me to her through my soft touch on her forehead. There were no words; time stood still. I was moved, as I felt she offered more to me than I did to her. Her presence was its own blessing. I felt humbled.

I took several deep breaths with her in this way, then bowed respectfully, moving aside to allow the next travel mate to enjoy a sublime moment with this gorgeous being. I found my way to a quiet corner to engage in my reverie, which included more tears. While there, I offered a silent prayer that all elephants may be allowed to remain in their native habitats. Or, if in the care of humans, they be always respected as the intelligent, noble, and powerful co-inhabitants of our precious earth.

CARRY THE LOAD

In 2012, we traveled to the coast of Panama and then upcountry to the beautiful mountain town of Boquete during their annual flower festival. While there, we visited a coffee plantation, zip-lined over the mountainous countryside, and hiked to a beautiful waterfall in the heart of the fertile and steamy Panamanian jungle.

We heard of a not-to-miss horseback ride through the mountains some distance from the town, so we signed up, hoping it was a respectful outfit that took care of their horses. We would join others for a two-hour ride through a diverse countryside.

Once we arrived, the honchos were very helpful as we mounted our horses. I was concerned, however, when they placed a rather large man on a medium-sized horse. This man did not seem to know how to ride.

Off we trotted into the most gorgeous countryside I have ever ridden in. Mountainous green rolling hills sprawled before us. A desert-like terrain morphed into a tropical landscape dotted with small palms. The flowing streams running through deep canyons irrigated the groves of leafy trees, where we paused to cool off in the shade. I would have loved to ride all day on my very responsive horse.

The large man on the medium-sized horse was having trouble. His horse did not want to move, no matter how hard he kicked with his heels. Finally, the guide had to lead the horse home by the reins, with the man still in the saddle. Horses always want to return to the stables, so I knew something was amiss.

I wondered if the horse was out of alignment. Years before, I had encountered a friend's Arabian horse, prone to bucking off all but small children. At the request of my friend, I examined the horse and found that the horse's lower back was out of alignment. After just one treatment, her ill-tempered horse became an easy ride.

When we returned to the stables, I explained my profession and respectfully asked if they would like me to check the horse for a possible lower back issue. I received a resounding "Por favor!"

I climbed aboard a mounting block to have a good look. This would also allow me the leverage needed to make a chiropractic correction. Sure enough, the horse's last lumbar and sacrum were out of alignment. I was surprised at how easy it was to articulate its spine back into place.

After correcting these alignment issues, I asked if I could check the other horses. A collective "Por favor!" resounded again. Very few of the horses had any significant issues. The men offered their gratitude with a "Mil gracias." I quietly hoped that if a horse resisted moving because of the weight of a hefty human, they would get that person off the horse.

The people I know who have horses care for them in the best way possible. They listen and tune in when they observe a problem. I am always grateful to be with horses, if only to pet and coo at them. I love their personas, strengths, and willingness to carry us humans around on their strong backs!

THE MIRACLE OF COWS

Many years ago, an LA stock trader had the good sense to quit his job and acquire 180 acres of land north of Santa Barbara. A 360-degree view rolled out from a palm-dotted oceanscape to a backcountry view that melted into the Santa Ynez Mountain range. The back end of this striking range included seven pyramidal peaks that cut into the distant skyline. He moved there with his wife and three kids to begin his life as a rancher.

A few years later, this rancher became a patient, a good friend, and a generous host to me and many other visitors I brought to his property. He eventually pared down to 90 acres of avocado and fruit trees. A small pond graced a lower canyon, and he established a year-round vegetable garden.

He also acquired some cows to complete the picture of ranch life. These half-dozen brown and black cows were free to roam on the remaining acreage of this sprawling property of rolling hills and descending verdant canyons. He spoiled them with daily doses of alfalfa and leftover fruits and vegetables from his orchard and garden.

One year, a miracle happened: a pure white male calf was born to a brown heifer and a brown bull. The veterinarian called it a one-in-a-million miracle. So, this young bull was named Milagro, which means miracle in Spanish. I was very eager to meet this miracle of nature.

The herd often gathered at the various gates, anticipating their next meal, or grazed in the lower pasture in the hollow below the property's cabana. We would journey in my friend's white pick-up, jumbling around in the back of the truck as we traversed up and down the many hilly roads to locate the herd.

It wasn't long before Mr. Milagro and I developed a bonded connection. I loved his scent: sagey, gamey, and full of bravado. He snorted and huffed when I rubbed his broad forehead and pet his growing girth. As he grew older and much bigger, he would often nose his way through the herd to receive his love pats.

Milagro did not take long to produce many other white "miracles." A few had a smattering of brown speckles on their hindquarters. Every calf was named, and the herd soon doubled. By age 13, Milagro got very thin and eventually took his last breath in a lower pasture. A younger look-alike bull was singled out and given the name Milagro II.

After a few years, my rancher friend firmly stated one day, "You have got to come to the ranch and tell Milagro what his new job is. We have not had any new calves in a while." Laughing, I immediately signed up for a long overdue visit to the ranch the following Saturday. I took my spouse with me to help with feeding time, which required us to throw thick flakes of alfalfa over a barbed wire fence to the eagerly awaiting herd.

We arrived late at the ranch, and feeding time was over. The cows were up the hill, contently grazing on weeds and scrabble. We scrambled up to the top to view the herd. Milagro II was grazing on the other side of the field.

Knowing I was there for a reason, I cupped my hands around my mouth.

"Milagro! Your boss here says you have a job to do! It is time to get on it!"

Jokes were made all around about my wording as Milagro glanced my way. I gesticulated towards all the female cows.

"Yeah, time to get busy!"

Satisfied I had done my part, we hiked back to the ranch house to enjoy lunch and catch up. The ranch's owner wasn't sure that Milagro had gotten the message. I assured him that nature would encourage that bull to do his duty.

About nine or so months later, my friend relayed to me that, finally, another white calf was born. Of course, I wanted to see it. We set a date for a meet and greet. Once at the ranch, we went to find and feed the cows. The calf was just weeks old, taking refuge under her mother. We threw some hay to the herd and congratulated Milagro II. He seemed smugly content with his work.

However, after viewing the girth of several of the brown females, I knew that even more calves were on the way. I mentioned this to my rancher friend. I even pointed out one Bessie I was sure was ready to calve any day.

It did not take long. Two weeks later, five more calves appeared in the herd, with the seventh one arriving two months later. We joked that Milagro certainly knew his job now. The boss thanked me!

More interesting to me was that on a subsequent visit, I again assisted in feeding the herd, now significantly reduced in size due to a transfer of cows to another owner. Once all the alfalfa, apples, and onions had been delivered, I ambled over to the fence to observe their feeding time.

Milagro II lifted his head from his lunch of hay and spotted me. He immediately pushed his way through the herd to where I was standing. He seemed to recognize me as he extended his head over the barbed fencing toward me. I scratched the broad spot between his ears and lovingly cleared the bramble off his face and eyes. His eyes closed just a bit with my nurturing affection. I could feel magic in the air.

When I hoisted myself back into the truck, I asked if this fully grown bull had let others pet him. My friend did not think so. I wondered aloud to the ranch owner this thought: perhaps human-to-animal positive—or negative—connections are passed from parent to offspring through their morphogenic fields, as proposed by Rupert Sheldrake. This might explain why subsequent generations of animals I have connected with in the wild allow me similar or enhanced connections with them.

No matter. I can continue enjoying this sweet new friendship with yet another Miracle in my life.

HORSES READ ENERGY

One beautiful summer afternoon, I ventured north with a friend to our mutual friend's horse ranch to celebrate her daughter's first birthday. I was as excited to be around the horses as I was to mingle with the invited celebrators.

We pulled up a dusty road and parked; I spied what looked like a barn and asked if I could say hello to the horses. My friend pointed the way, so I strode to the barn for a meet and greet. Eight horses were stabled there. As I moved from stall to stall, I reached out to pet each one. They all ignored me. "Well," I thought, "who am I anyway to them?" Nonetheless, I was surprised that no one wanted a scratch around the ears. So, I ambled over to the guests gathering around the young one and her parents.

Over the course of the event, I learned that two horses were not doing well. One was owned by a friend whom I had not seen in decades. The other was a mini horse that could barely walk. After explaining my profession, I asked both owners if they wanted me to check out their babies. They nodded their consent.

The mini horse was gentle and subdued, no doubt in pain. Many parts of its whole body were out of alignment, and I applied direct but subtle force in those areas until I felt its spine and hips were aligned. They then took their baby for a ten-minute walk. Thankfully, it appeared to be doing better. I hoped for the best, as I could see how distressed the owners were for their baby.

I was about to leave when my friend from many years ago headed back to the barn to attend to her horse. It had a skin condition that made it very painful to be touched. I asked her if she wanted me to apply one of my energic healing techniques to see if I could assist the horse in its healing process. She said yes.

I noticed that the horse appeared to have some form of infection and that its immune system was not responding well. I quietly worked on the horse without touching its skin. It took all of ten minutes.

The horse in the stall behind me now began stomping his foot on a metal bar at the bottom of the stall's door. He kept doing this until I turned around to see about the racket. He looked directly at me and stamped his foot again. I started laughing. "Oh, now you want some attention from me. Uh-huh." As I was done with the healing on my friend's horse, I turned to attend the stomper. He extended his head to me for pats and pets, almost demanding that I give him plenty of attention.

Soon, the pretty lady horse next to him began to push her head into his stall so I could pet her. I laughed and shook my head at their antics. But the exciting thing I noted was that they somehow could see the energy flowing to the other horse and wanted a piece of the action. It spoke to their personalities and horsey intelligence.

Too soon, it was time to leave. I promised the horses I would return someday for another visit. Months later, I checked with my friend about the mini. It turned out that the mini could now walk pain-free. I also reached out to the other horse's owner. It turns out her horse's condition healed as well.

Grateful that they were better, I hoped I had contributed to their healing. But the real story was that those other two horses could read the energy and made sure I knew they wanted in on the action. I am still shaking my head and smiling to this day.

13

IT ALL BEGAN AT HOME

Dogs and cats around the globe have worked their magic to show humans how to open their hearts to unconditional love. Perhaps many of us love our animal companions even more than other humans, as our pets do not often voice their true thoughts about our human faults. Every cat or dog that enters my path will receive an outstretched hand or a welcoming pat of love. I have learned innumerable lessons about the Field from the beautiful animals that have graced my life since childhood.

Throughout the years, my pets have taught me the true nature of unconditional love. As a child, we were always fortunate to have dogs and cats who could mediate the chaos of our family of eight with their humorous antics and unfiltered affection for us.

My mom always had a way with animals and treated them like one of her children. Her only problem was how short their lives were. After losing a beloved pet, she would swear never to get another. After sufficient time had passed, I would remind her that she would give some stray a beautiful life by taking them under her wing. She always relented and would soon manifest the next family pet that needed a loving home.

JEFÈ COMES UP WITH A PLAN

Through Jefe (Spanish for "chief"), I learned that dogs could be intuitive and intelligent. Jefe, a mix between Shepard and Irish Setter, was not only handsome but very smart. My mom would direct him to get a late sleeper up, and off he would saunter to dutifully fulfill his task. Jefe was a true family dog and extended his love to all of us. He was also a problem solver.

One afternoon, when we were away, he got stranded in the house and desperately needed to relieve himself. He was not the kind of dog to lift a leg in the house. One can only imagine how he came up with his solution. Somehow, he aimed perfectly and filled his dog bowl to the brim to find relief. He received copious praise, petting, and treats —after my dad carefully emptied and washed out his grub bowl!

14

DEVA, THE ONCE HUMAN

When I finally settled into my career as a chiropractor, I knew it was time to find the perfect dog. It did not take long.

In the mid-1980s, I traveled up to the Sierras, where I met an elite runner with a knack for procuring exceptional Golden Retrievers. This was my favorite dog breed, and I was excited to connect with her dog, Koa. In the short time I visited their mountain retreat, I became attached to this athletic beauty of a dog, who tolerated my hugs and pets more than she would other people. I implored my new friend to allow Koa to have puppies so that I could adopt one. She indicated that she and her husband were thinking of breeding her.

Time passed, and I received word that Koa was pregnant and expected to deliver in September. I put in my request, as I knew that I wanted a female dog. I pondered aloud what I should name her. I had recently read a missive on devas, or nature spirits. That seemed like the perfect name.

Koa gave birth to seven puppies, and pictures soon followed. One of the female puppies was dubbed "The Divine Miss M." I mused that the names Deva and Divine were similar enough; this was a sign of which dog to choose. Twelve weeks later, I made the trip up to the mountain retreat to meet my new animal companion in life. Not surprisingly, it was love at first sight. She was a light golden color with the perfect coat, paws, and adoring eyes. We immediately bonded.

She was also a very smart doggie. Even as a puppy, she understood English. On our first unleashed walk together, we came to a stoplight. I told her to sit and wait. She did as commanded. From that moment on, I rarely had her on a leash, except when required.

Deva managed to amuse me nonstop. On one trip back to the mountain retreat, Little Deva, Koa, and her cousin, Emmy Lou, joined us as we cross-country skied in the backcountry. She followed behind Koa, watching as her mama padded only in our ski tracks. On one sparkling winter's day, we humans decided to practice our telemark skiing downhill, so we climbed to an accessible knoll above a trail. The dogs trekked up to the top, sinking into the deep snow. After watching us for ten minutes, they decided to get in on the action. With her head facing downhill, Koa rolled onto her back and wiggled her way down the slope. Deva and Emmy Lou watched with tales wagging, and soon, the three of them were sliding headfirst down the hill, wiggling, and barking in pure joy. We gave up our attempts to practice telemarking to watch the three retrievers' antics. Deva so enjoyed this maneuver that in the years to come, she would repeat this antic on snow drifts or thick piles of leaves on hillsides. From this precious being, I learned the art of doing something just for the pure joy of it.

Once Deva got a little older, I spent three weeks teaching her to sit and come on command. She quickly learned to "roll over," "give me a paw," and would retrieve anything. For fun, I trained her to balance a stick or treat on her nose, fling it into the air on command, and then catch it in one graceful movement.

She grew into her beautiful sienna red coat, with a well-proportioned face and a strong body. She had personality, wit, compassion, and a fabulous playfulness that engaged many of my friends. She was not interested in other dogs but worked hard to maintain her relationships with her human pals.

We would travel everywhere together. When downtown, I would have her wait for me in the doorway of a store. She soon learned what stores she could sneak into to find me. Once found, I would be joyously greeted until I escorted her back to her post outside.

Deva lived up to the retriever part of her breed. She was obsessed with fetching, especially at the beach. Once we were settled on our towel, she would snoop around for the perfect piece of driftwood. It had to have heft.

She then turned her attention to the shoreline for possible playmates. Once located, she would race toward them and drop her stick directly in their path. If the person complied by picking up the stick and throwing it, they were her forever friends. She would continue with them on their beach walk, redeposit the driftwood at their feet, then fetch again, ad infinitum. When her play pals grew weary of the game, she merely transferred her enthusiasm to the next beach walker, coaxing them into participating in her life passion.

WHEN DOGS SEEM HUMAN

In the early part of our life together, two psychics told me--at different times--that Deva had been a human before she was a dog. For the life of me, I couldn't understand why she would want to come back as a dog, given the shorter lifespan. Over time, I figured it out: she didn't have to work, she was lovingly fed healthy food, she could play with pure enthusiasm and joy, and she was loved and respected by friends and family. In other words, she got a break, perhaps, from life's travails. Observing how much love I extend to my animals, many friends have expressed, "Next time, I am coming back as your dog,"

Deva was a talker. Perhaps because she had been human, she understood the human language and process of communication. When I would come home from work, she had a series of woofs and barks that said, very clearly, "Where the heck have you been?"

or "It is time for a walk," or "I need a treat." I learned dog language from her over the years and always knew what she communicated.

I often took her to work, where she would sit in my open van in the shade by the front door. From there, she would greet her fan club. She was very popular. She would converse with people who seemed to understand her in her doggie language.

Deva acquired a "boyfriend" whom she loved madly. This tall, blond, athletic, Danish thirty-something did not have a dog, so he would ask to borrow Deva for beach time. To her delight, they would go for long runs on the beach, and he would endlessly throw sticks for her. My only stipulation was that he bathed her with the outdoor hose after their time at the beach.

Deva was, in every sense of the word, a water dog. But when it came to getting a bath, she would run to the furthest outpost of the yard and cower. I had to drag her across the yard for bath time. Her Danish boyfriend would turn on the water full blast and say, "Deva, come here." She would crawl over to him with deep trust and undying love, shivering with fear of the "Dreaded Hose." She would shake herself dry and follow him around until he departed, always forlorn for an hour afterward.

Deva was always eager to make friends and cultivate a special relationship with them. She uniquely greeted each friend with a bark, a kiss, or a paw. She commanded a "hello" from any visitor, even in her later years when she could not get up to greet them.

She was quite the athlete most of her life and would accompany me on many of my long workouts. She learned to follow verbal directions while we biked together, such as, "Turn right" or "Wait at the corner." She loved to swim next to me in the ocean (barking furiously if I got ahead of her). She ran by my side in local evening foot races by the sea. She was my co-triathlete—if only she were fast enough to keep me competitive.

She also willingly pulled me on my rollerblades along our town's oceanfront bike path. There was no better companion for hiking on our many gorgeous local trails. In other words, Deva was my perfect athletic companion.

DEVA INVENTS NEW GAMES

Deva was a great self-entertainer. She could discover joy in any number of activities. She often inspired me and others to engage in her playful activities. But sometimes, I had to draw the line.

One spring, I took a group of students to Sedona to camp by a meandering creek to enjoy a spiritual retreat together. I drove there with Deva riding shotgun in the front seat. Once there, she began bothering the retreaters with barking pleas to play fetch.

I took her aside and told her that our time in the desert wasn't centered around her needs. I told her she would have to entertain herself as we had spiritual work to do. I saw her take this in; immediately, her wheels began to turn. She would figure out a way to have fun.

A few hours later, we sojourned to a beautiful babbling brook to lounge in the sun in quiet contemplation. Deva realized from my stern look that she was required to self-entertain during our time there.

She waded into the cool water, looking for something to play with. She picked up a rock, looked at me, and dropped it into the stream. It sank! She poked her head underwater with her eyes open to fetch the rock. She soon gave up on this pastime.

Deva then located a hefty broken pine bow, hauled it from the wooded area, and dropped it into the stream. She watched it meander down the creek, then eagerly swam to retrieve it. Yet the log moved too slowly for her taste. I observed her contemplating how to make it more challenging. She panted, excited that she had figured out how to entertain herself.

A bit later, we all scrambled up to a flat ledge that overlooked the flowing stream. Deva followed us there and looked around for a new game. She acquired a new stick a yard long and as wide as her open mouth and dragged it over to the edge of the ledge. With both paws on it, Deva pretended that someone was trying to wrestle it away from her. She battled that imaginary foe for a minute or two, then glanced away as she nonchalantly flipped the stick over the ledge, where it hit the stream with a splash.

Deva looked up at us, then at the stream, feigning shock that the stick had gotten away from her. Indignant, she jumped up and watched as her toy burbled away, captured by the creek's flow. When it was a challenging distance away, Deva leaped five feet through the air into the stream and began paddling furiously toward her prize. My precious pup made a big show of rescuing the stick, then swam upstream to return to her spot on the flat rock. She then shook and showered us amidst our squeals. Deva repeated this exact process many times, much to everyone's amusement. Finally worn out, she took a well-earned snooze on the sunny rock, as did the rest of her retreat mates. As her mamma, I was impressed with my doggie's creative self-recreation effort.

DEVA GOES FOR IT

One warm summer day, Deva and I hiked up to Seven Falls in the high hills of Santa Barbara. After greeting everyone sunning themselves at the falls, Deva immediately took off to explore the area. She soon found herself stranded on top of a ten-foot waterfall, with no way for me to rescue her. The fellow hikers sitting around the pool below were concerned for her safety. We brainstormed together on how to assist Deva in escaping her predicament.

After some quick thinking, I procured a large, inviting stick to throw into the pool below. That retriever would not be able to resist fetching it. I hoisted the perfect instrument of temptation and waved it in the air. My darling dog's attention locked onto it immediately. I tossed the stick into the air with a smooth arch so that it would land in the lower pool. Ms. Deva looked at me, then at the flotilla, then back at me. "Go get it!" I urged her.

Deva edged her way to the brink of the waterfall and peered down at the bobbling stick. Gathering courage and momentum, she sprang off the upper pool's slight outcrop, plunging into the chilly water below with one big splash. When Deva came to the surface, her prize protruding from either side of her mouth, we all exhaled in relief. She paddled over to the rock-lined shore, gleaming with pride. Once on land, Ms. Deva gloriously shook herself dry, exhilarated by the cheers erupting from her fellow hikers. I was one proud mom.

DEVA SPEAKS HER MIND

The time came to get a second dog, which we hoped would assuage our grief when the inevitable day would come for Deva to depart this earth. We loaded her into the van and headed to the shelter.

Upon arriving at the pound, the volunteer took us around to view the possible adoptees. This woman was a real pro, extolling each dog's unseen virtues. As we toured the facility, none of the dogs seemed to be the one. Finally, I pointed to a blonde lab-pit mix with pointed ears that folded over at the tips, deep clear brown eyes, maybe 4-5 years old. "What about that one?" Our pound escort jumped at the possibility of securing an adoption for this pit mix.

After taking him for a brief walk, we walked him to my van to meet Deva. The doors were wide open, and he jumped in before I could stop him. Deva, very protective of her van, did not bite his head off but instead greeted him cordially. Though not entirely sold on this rescue, we thought, "Well... he'll do."

We signed release papers, noting that the previous owners gave up the dog due to their inability to pay the fines. That should have been a clue.

Within a few hours at his new home, this rogue of a dog tore up Deva's favorite, well-cared-for sheepskin ball. He snapped at her when she lovingly welcomed him to our home with a dog kiss. Deva reacted with a hurt expression on her face, turning away. I was concerned; this new addition's behavior did not bode well for integrating him into our household.

After a few days of observing their disconnect, we decided to sit them down for a family meeting. With my hands on both dogs, I looked at one, then the other with concern. I politely said, "Doggies, we are a family now and want you both to get along."

Well, Deva could hold her tongue no longer. Looking into my eyes, she howled three jaw-articulating distinct sentences, "He chewed up my favorite toy! Then, he snapped at me!" She lowered her head. "Wasn't I good enough that you had to bring home another dog?" she whimpered. She continued emoting with wailing cries. We did our best not to laugh as we tightly hugged her. I assured her that she was my "best doggie ever" and that I would love her to the end. With a deep sniffle, she went to her bed and let it go.

While the two dogs were never best friends, they co-existed peacefully for their remaining years together.

DEVA NEEDS A HELPING HAND

By age twelve, Deva's athletic endeavors were catching up to her. At times, she could barely walk due to a lumbar disc issue. Her spirit still wanted to run, though. I almost bought her a doggie wagon for her rear legs. I knew I could not keep my good dog down.

I wondered if she would let me lift her by her tail while on our walks. The first time I tried it, she glanced back at me momentarily and, because her pain eased, sprinted down the street as I scrambled alongside her to keep up. After that, we took spirited ambles around the neighborhood and even took short hikes together. I did get dirty looks walking her downtown in this manner.

Retrievers are famous for being water dogs. My water pooch and I continued swimming in the ocean well into her advanced years. While in the water, Deva could paddle quite well with minimal pain. She and I swam to the buoys off our favorite beach's coast on her thirteenth birthday. Once there, we visited an anchored sailboat, where the sailors heartedly congratulated Deva's spry spirit. Two years later, we enjoyed one last beautiful birthday swim.

My lesson in observing the many adventures of Deva was always this: "Where there is a will, there is a way."

DEVA'S SPIRIT MOVES ON

Deva's spirit was so strong that she survived the removal of thirteen cancerous tumors in two separate operations at ages 11 and 13. She rallied heartily and could even walk better after her second surgery.

At some point, Deva appeared to be succumbing to more cancer. Sad and worried, I took her to our veterinarian, my heart breaking. He examined her and said, "I think it might be time." It was not the right moment for me, and I asked if we could wait a few days so I could have time with her at home to say goodbye. He thought it would be okay to wait a few days.

Deva and I lay by the fire that night, my arms around her. I spoke to her in low, soothing tones. I asked her if it was her time to go. She immediately sent me a picture of one of my good friends, who was a powerful healer. Two other friends' images appeared in my mind. I thought that Deva just wanted to say goodbye to these beloved friends.

The following day, I awoke with the pictures of these women appearing in my consciousness. I knew I had to call them. They all immediately agreed to stop by our home. My first friend came and placed healing hands on her. The next woman performed a Reiki healing on her. The last one lovingly talked to Deva as she sweetly petted her for an hour.

The next day, Deva had improved significantly. Two days later, I had our vet check her vitals, and he agreed that she looked much better and that it was not her time to go. Relief flooded through my body.

As we drove away from our consultation with him, I realized Deva had specifically asked our healer friends to visit her for their healing talents. For the next nine months, she seemed happy and content to lay on her bed and greet all visitors to the house with a resounding series of "Woof, woof, woofs," which translated to, "Come say hi to me first!"

This best friend of a dog lived until she was almost sixteen years old. When her time seemed close, I took Deva into my home office and lay on the floor with her. As I wrapped my arms around her, she struggled to breathe. I looked into her eyes as tears welled up in mine. "I want you to stay as long as you can but let me know when you're your time to go." I knew she would need assistance with her passing; this broke my heart.

As night was surrendering to the coming dawn, Deva pawed desperately at my door, struggling even harder to breathe. Realizing this was the moment, I tumbled out of bed, threw on my clothes, and carried her down the stairs to the car. We both drove her to the emergency hospital, grimacing at the sound of her labored breathing.

She was lovingly escorted to the 'other side' at dawn's first morning light by the ministrations of a compassionate veterinarian. We appreciated his soothing and kind manner.

There was a moment of accepting peace for Deva's now resolved suffering, and then a torrent of grief burst forth. I sobbed my way back to the car. Through my tears, I reflected that Deva had lived life to her absolute fullest. I comforted myself, knowing I would always treasure the life we had shared over our fifteen years together.

Once home, I drifted off to sleep at 5 AM as the sun peeked through an orange and reddened horizon. A dream image flashed into my consciousness of a red-tailed hawk lifting off into the sunrise, free from the burden of this earthly realm. I silently wept again and knew I would feel the void of her presence in my life for a long time. I then fell into a deep slumber, my heart knowing I would awaken to a house empty of her loving exuberance. This is the price we pay for the unconditional love we share with our beloved pets during their journey with us. It is worth it.

DEVA RETURNS TO EARTH?

A few months later, I had a dream about Deva. In this lucidly clear dream, I walked across a patio and noticed Deva lying in a slight depression in the dirt. She was still, and as I approached her, I thought she had passed on. I bent down to gaze at her, I thought, in her final resting place. My hand reached out to pet her coat, once my refuge and solace. In shock, I saw her twitch - she was alive! I was overjoyed.

I reverently collected her in my arms. She was light and easy to carry across the patio. I shooed people out of the way, saying, "She's alive! Deva's alive!" I felt vulnerable yet unconditionally loving and accepting of whatever was to happen next.

I then carried her the short distance to the other side of the patio. When I looked down at her in my arms again, she was now a newborn human baby. I paused and then tenderly decided to do everything to make her comfortable. I tightly swaddled her in a cloth, thinking this would greatly comfort her. She did not cry. I showed her to my mother and held her tight against my body, as much a comfort to me.

When I woke from this dream, I acutely felt in my soul that Deva had already taken the next step by returning to this earthly plane as a baby girl. As I ruminated about the dream, I burst into sobs, realizing that I was afraid that Deva had, by all odds, come back into this world without the comforts I now know. For a moment, I feared that my blessed doggie had been born into hardship, as so many human children do, without proper food, warmth, or safety. With that thought, I shed tears for all the world's children.

When I finally arose from my morning reverie, I loaded my other dog, Rune, into the back of the car for a trek up a mountain road. On our way home, I spied a golden retriever behind a fence, tail wagging, sporting an enthusiastic grin from ear to ear. I imagined it was Deva, appearing to me one last time to reassure me that she was doing fine. This lifted my spirit to a deeper, more profound experience of acceptance and joy.

15

RUNE, THE PEOPLE WHISPERER

ADOPTING A BAD BOY DOGGIE

We adopted Rune when he was around five years old. A blond hunk of a dog, Rune had a handsome yellow lab coat and tail and a white blaze on his chest. His large, pointed ears folded down, giving him his ready-for-action aura.

During our first meeting, he was friendly and seemed ready to please with the easy wag of his tail. We took him out for a spin around the adoption center, and he did well on a leash. Deva greeted him in our car with no complaint. He seemed like the perfect fit for our household. Little did we know that he was a rogue and an escape artist.

Rune's initial integration into our household was less than stellar. He was reprimanded when he snapped at Deva's welcoming kiss, he chewed up her sheepskin ball with no consequence and lunged at Mr. Guy, our beloved Russian Blue cat.

His finishing touch was lifting his leg onto the antique hutch to mark this new abode as his. All of this happened in the first hour of being with us. With a stern look, I threatened Rune with an eminent return to the slammer.

We took a deep breath, looked at each other, and wondered what we had gotten ourselves into.

Mr. Rune was not done with our initiation. An hour later, the front door opened momentarily, and our precious new pooch did what any respectable freed dog would do: he bolted down the steps, across the driveway, and galloped full speed down the street.

The salt in the wound was that glance over his shoulder as we desperately called after him. We both swore we heard him say, "Yeah, right! See ya!"

Frantic, we called the pound. Our volunteer answered the phone and consoled us by assuring us that she would not charge us this first time when they picked him up. With trepidation, we asked how much it would cost after that, "Fifty dollars," she replied. This could get expensive.

We got him back in a few hours and immediately purchased dog tags. It was a good call, as Rune bolted often. He would take off down the street, cross a busy road, and run until he found a place to hang out for the day. All he required for his hangout were senior citizens with treats, other 'cool' dogs to roughhouse with, or children, as he loved kids. Typically, we would get a phone call at the end of the day, "Could you please come to pick up your dog? He's been here all day." When we asked why they waited so long to call, we would hear, "Oh, but he was playing so nicely with the children that we didn't want to interrupt them."

A month after adopting Rune, I came home and discovered that he was excommunicated to the front deck. He had chewed a hole the size of a plate into the back of our new sheepskin seat cover—good reason for some time out.

With hands on hips, I walked out to the deck and gave him a stern look. Somewhat rhetorically, I asked, "Rune, whatever were you thinking?"

He looked at me and instantly transmitted a picture of the sheepskin ball he had chewed up—no big deal.

"But Rune, that was a toy; this was a brand-new seat cover." I retorted.

He shot me a glance. Then, clear as a bell, I heard a voice in my head. "Nowwwww, you tell me." He looked away, indignant.

Oh my gosh, this dog can send thoughts. Really? Shaking my head with amusement, I laughed and forgave him instantly. But I kept him out on the deck a bit longer to let him know who the boss was here.

THE CAAAAAT

A year later, Mr. Guy, our beloved Russian Blue, departed this earthly plane. After a few months, we casually talked about adding a new cat to the household, which we now called the Funny Farm.

At my parent's house that weekend, a young black cat with no collar appeared on the courtyard wall, sweetly taunting Rune and my parents' dogs with his charming antics. Because I love black cats, I pushed through the barking dogs to pet the cat on the wall, who seemed undisturbed by the ruckus. The cat even followed me to the street curb where we could commune in a mutual lovefest, observed from afar by the dogs at the gate. I later asked everyone if we should take the cat home with us. We were immediately informed that the cat belonged to the neighbors next door. Too bad.

That night at home, Rune, clearly agitated, followed me from room to room. All I could hear in my head was, "The CAAAT, the CAAAT!" It took me a while to realize that Rune was stressing about the black cat. Apparently, he had read my mind about wanting to bring the young black cat home with us. I looked down at Rune and said, "Rune, we are not bringing that cat home!" He stopped following me and retired to his bed.

The next morning, he followed me again, projecting his concern into my thoughts.

"The caaat, the caaat!"

I stopped in my tracks to address him. "Rune. There is no cat. Now let it go."

He paused, looked at me, and, finally satisfied, padded off to his dog bed.

RUNE'S FORMER LIFE

Hiking with Rune could be a real pain. Watching him on the trail with other dogs, I imagined he fancied himself a macho warrior. He wanted to take on any dog we would meet; the bigger, the better. He even mistook a horse for a giant dog—until he sprang up close enough to the horse's mouth to realize his mistake. Small dogs meant nothing to him; he would not give them the time of day.

Once, after one of his snarling episodes, I stopped him, made him sit, and asked him why he was so aggressive with other dogs. A picture of a Chinese warrior popped into my head. I could see an ancient countryside before me, with rugged mountain passes in the background. Was this Rune's past life as an Asian fighter? I decided to do a healing for him right there on the trail. I made him sit and be still.

During this session, he relayed to me with detailed pictures that his sensei had commanded him to kill his best friend. He followed this horrific order but, being guilt-ridden, sacrificed himself in battle soon after. He forever condemned himself to "the life of a dog."

I just stared at him. I could feel his pain. I could sense I needed to help him clear his guilt and deep regret. After a few minutes of processing, he appeared to let it all go with a significant and vocal yawn.

You might think that I imagined this whole story about Rune. But a strange thing happened after he unburdened his soul to me. He stopped attacking dogs. Instead, at my behest, he went around them peacefully. But his transformation did not end there.

As it turned out, he began to take his spiritual evolution seriously.

RUNE EVOLVES

Soon after, Rune began to develop a compassionate nature. One winter night, we came home to find our bedroom fleeced in white. Gracie, our newest young canine addition, had torn up a prized new silk pillow and covered the entire bed and room with its contents. When we scolded her for the mess, she ran to the living room and cowered in the corner.

I dragged her into the bedroom to survey the damages. "Gracie, why did you do this?" She glanced up, humiliated, and I distinctly heard a small, high voice say, "It made me feel better." Understanding that she suffered from separation anxiety, I paused, knowing there should be some consequence. "You go downstairs and take a time out." She scooted out the back door and down the rear stairs, plunging under the deck below to her "cave of shame."

That night, I needed to sleep in the living room as I was getting over a cold. Gracie and Rune considered themselves the guardians of our household and, therefore, slept near the front door. When it was time for lights out, I went to the back door and called Gracie to come up and go to bed. Still ashamed, she stayed ensconced in her cave. "Fine," I said, "Suit yourself."

After shutting the lights out, I went to my mat to sleep. Moments later, there was a paw on my arm. It was Rune.

"What, Rune."

"Get Gracie."

"I already called her." There was that paw on my arm again.

"Cold."

Pause. "Right. Okay, Rune. I'll get her."

I got up and called into the darkness for Gracie. No response. I paused, wondering what would get her back in the house. I then called out, "Who wants a treat?"

With a jangle of her collar, Gracie bounded up the backstairs. With my hands on my hips, I said, "Your treat is that you get to sleep inside tonight with Rune. Now get to bed." She darted to her nightly station and settled down with a harrumph. Within moments, with everyone tucked in, Rune expressed a contented sigh. Soon, we were all asleep.

RUNE LEARNS TO MEDITATE

One spring morning, I stood in our lower courtyard when Rune trundled down the back stairs. He sat directly in front of me and projected a focused intent. I glanced down, curious. He put his right paw on my thigh.

"What? I have fed you, walked you, and you have water in your bowl."

Again, he pawed my thigh. I closed my eyes, tuned in, then heard his request.

"I want to be spiritual."

"You want to be spiritual?"

He shifted back and forth from leg to leg while his ears pitched forward, looking very earnest. We called this maneuver the Runie Dance.

With an acknowledging nod, I said, "Okay, Rune, how about now?"

I led him to our redwood deck, ablaze with the midmorning sun's warmth, and we lay down together, side-by-side. Within minutes, we each fell into a profound meditation lasting for a half hour. Afterward, I realized I often felt a deep inner silence around Rune.

A week later, Rune appeared before me and earnestly performed his Runie Dance again.

"What, Rune?"

"Can I come tonight?"

That night, I was hosting our weekly meditation class. I stared at him momentarily, wondering how he knew we were gathering. I generally don't allow our pets to attend classes, as they can be charmingly disruptive. But how could I say no?

"You may come, but you must stay in the kitchen."

Satisfied with my answer, he lumbered off for a nap.

That night, Rune was on board to greet the students. When the class started, I gave him "the look," and he padded off to the kitchen. Once there, he placed his crossed paws over the threshold and attentively focused on me during class. When it was time for us to meditate, he closed his eyes and appeared to fall into a deep meditation.

Over the next several weeks, Rune humbly asked permission to join our class on Monday nights. I always said yes. Week by week, he crept closer to our circle until he was in the living room with us all. He would listen intently to the teachings, then stretch out on the rug during meditation time.

One evening, as the group was standing in a circle holding hands, Rune decided that he wanted to join the group in a meaningful way. He nosed into our circle by wiggling between a tall student's legs. Everyone welcomed his enthusiastic participation. Beaming his big Runie grin, he looked around at everyone, thrilled to finally be recognized as a group member.

From that point on, upon waking, Rune would gallop through the house from his guardian post into the bedroom, leaping onto the bed to have a 10-minute meditation with me before I rose for the day. He would snuggle in, close his eyes, and engage in inner silence with me. It was divine for both of us.

Several months after his initiation into the group, I held a weekend workshop at our home on "Manifesting Your Intentions." In the days leading up to the seminar, Rune followed me around the house, expressing excitement about the workshop. Would he be allowed to attend? Why not?

He greeted everyone at the front door on the first evening of our event. When I asked the workshop participants about Rune joining us, they sweetly accepted his interest in attending. Once we gathered, he took his place on the rug, just behind where I offered my presentation. He stayed the whole evening.

On the morning of the last day, students were asked to put their intentions for manifestation on paper. I would place these in a box, and then collectively, we would engage in a group intention empowerment meditation.

During my morning meditation with Rune, the thought, "I want to put an intention in the box," passed through my mind. I opened my eyes and glanced over at Rune.

"What is your intention then, Rune?"

"To be more spiritual," he transmitted. I nodded.

"Okay, Rune, I will write it out for you and put it in the box."

He smiled with his eyes.

This time, Rune joined our circle on the rug, facing inwards and looking around at everyone. I explained to the group that I was also adding Rune's request. This elicited smiles from the participants.

We closed our eyes and began our manifestation meditation, which lasted thirty minutes. Afterward, each meditator shared their experience. One member stated that during the process, she saw a pair of blond dog paws extend toward the box. We all knew whose paws those were.

From then on, Rune steadily evolved as a dog and a spiritual being.

RUNE OPENS TO LOVE

I would be remiss if I didn't include Rune's grand love affair with Bella.

Bella fell in love with Rune when she came to live with us at the ripe old age of 14. A blue-gray tortoise with wildly fluffy fur, we sometimes called her Mrs. Cross for the perpetual scowl on her Persian face. Rune would have nothing to do with her because she was a caaaaat.

Bella would follow Rune around and attempt to share his meals — only to be met with a snarl. She'd sneak onto his dog bed at night, only to have him get up and move. Patiently, she persisted.

One Valentine's night, I decided to play Cupid. Rune was luxuriating next to a roaring fire. I lay down next to him for a "mamma cuddle." Soon, Bella sauntered over, looking amorously at Rune. He started to get up, but I intervened and pushed him back onto the rug. I then picked up Bella and placed her on Rune's reclining body. I petted both simultaneously while speaking in loving tones. Rune gradually relaxed and allowed Bella her purring sprawl across his body.

From that moment on, he would share his beloved meal with Ms. Bella. She only indulged in a few bites, of course. He allowed her to snuggle with him on his bed, but only after she had groomed his face and ears. When I would witness this nightly ritual, Rune would throw me a look. "I am only doing this for you." Right, Rune.

In time, it was clear that they were both committed to sleeping together on his dog bed. Their romance continued for many years, as Bella lived to be over nineteen. But, as she got thinner, I wondered when her time would come to leave us.

She might have chosen the night she wanted to leave us for the other worlds. It was a warm September night. Windows were left open to cool the house. Bella was indoors when I returned home from an end-of-summer concert. Later that night, I heard coyote yips and howls down the street, a bit too close for comfort. I never dreamed our dear cat would venture outside to the front driveway. But she did, and sadly, fell prey to some wild animal.

Later, in the early hours after midnight, a ghostlike grey mist appeared in our dimly lit bathroom. Spooky as it seemed then, upon later reflection, we surmised it was Bella, there to offer her goodbyes before leaving this world.

We feared the worst when Bella did not appear for breakfast. Rune stood in the hallway by the bathroom, forlorn, looking for his Bella. This was our second clue that something had happened to her. We finally found her body a few days later under a deck. To celebrate her long life, we held a formal burial in the front garden, with both dogs in attendance. They kept a somber watch as we lowered her into the earth. I sensed they knew she was gone.

From then on, Rune slept on the bathroom floor every night, even through the duration of the cold winter that followed. Perhaps he was hoping for her to return. After a year, he finally gave up his vigil and assumed his nightly post by the front door.

RUNE MOVES ON

Towards his later years, Rune communicated to me that he wanted to leave the earthly plane. "Just one more year," I begged. He silently agreed, even a bit reluctantly, as he put his head down with a sigh. Friends would visit Rune while he hung out quietly in the front bedroom. They would emerge from their audience with him and pull me aside to tell me, "Rune just told me that he wants to leave soon." I would respond, "I know, we had this discussion earlier this week," and then reassure them that he'd agreed to stay on the planet a while longer.

Rune never appeared to age. Yet, after he turned 15, he developed tumors and suffered from advanced arthritis. Several times, I thought we had lost him to a seizure, and yet, he would come back into consciousness and seem as present as ever.

After Christmas that year, it became clear that it was his time to go. He was having seizures, even on our walks together. With a heavy heart, I scheduled the appointment with our beloved veterinarian. I then reached out to Rune's loved ones to come over to offer their goodbyes.

When my brother arrived, we hung out with Rune in the lower courtyard on his comfy dog bed. We lay on the ground next to him and fed him beef tacos by hand. He was ever so present and alive with us. I could not believe it was his time. My heart was once again breaking from losing a dear pet.

When it was time to get Rune into the car, I stood up and looked at my "Bubby Boy." I burst into a distraught wail of "Noooooo." Rune struggled to rise from his dog bed, then hobbled over to me. He lifted one paw onto my thigh, looked up into my teary eyes, and clearly transmitted his final message, "It's okay, Mommy." He then turned, limped over to the gate, and waited patiently for me to regain my composure enough to lift him gently into the back of our station wagon.

It was a sad ride down the coast to our vet's office on that last day of the year. I somehow held back my tears, wanting to be strong for all of us. It was even more difficult because Rune did not appear to be in pain. I hoped we were doing the right thing.

When we arrived at the veterinarian's office, Rune knew to head to the back entrance for his last procedure. He calmly went to his destiny, facing it without fear. We left the vet's office devastated, again facing the visceral void when a beloved pet must go. We gathered with Rune's loved ones on the beach that night to celebrate his life and the year's end with a small bonfire and sweet memories of a being who opened to love and spiritual evolution. He left a void in my heart that will never be filled.

RUNE'S FINAL MIRACLE

Rune appeared several times in my dreams to comfort me, looking alive and well. His final offering, though, was nothing short of a miracle.

One night, many months after Rune had passed, I stopped and stared at his picture on our refrigerator, my heart saddened by his absence. I then proceeded to my home office to finish up some work. Feeling unsettled, I got up to gaze at his portrait hanging on the wall behind me. He looked handsome and dapper in a top hat and silk tie.

A heavy-hearted sigh escaped from my lips. Hearing this, my spouse entered the office and stood behind me, asking what was wrong. I pointed to Rune's picture and tearfully said, "I miss our boy." We stood in silence, feeling the emptiness of his presence in the household.

A moment later, the lights in the adjoining room blacked out completely, followed by a loud rattling crash. We turned to look for the source of the disturbance. A tackle box of beads was on the floor, somehow still intact, at the base of the computer cupboard. That bead box had been safely stowed at the back of its shelf. We both stared at it in disbelief as the cupboard doors remained tightly closed.

I stared suspiciously at the downed box, wondering how it propelled itself off its shelf and through the cupboard doors. My mind was unable to resolve how this mysterious occurrence had happened. Instead, I chuckled softly and shook my head.

"Okay, Rune, I get it. You want us to know that you are still with us." I then sensed his presence in the room, and my sadness dissipated. Later, I contemplated his spirited journey from "bad boy doggie" to evolving into a beautifully soulful being. To this day, I miss hearing Rune gallop through the house to jump in bed for his morning meditation cuddle or his endearing and expressive "Runie Dance."

Those of you who have pets know that the love, humor, and memories we share with these extraordinary beings are a gorgeous treasure in our lives. My fondest wish is that the story of Rune, the human whisperer, will inspire you to listen quietly for the thoughts that your pets may have to share with you, their absolute beloveds.

They know more than we will ever realize.

16

THE HEALING IN THE FIELD

After we lost Deva, my partner had a vision of a reddish shepherd-lab mix one morning. Her name was to be Gracie. It did not take long for us to find her through a dog rescuer in Big Bear. She was six months old when we got her and very shy. With love and encouragement, she quickly integrated into our household.

GRACIE'S MIRACLE HEALING

One bright Saturday afternoon, while bathing Gracie, I noticed a large half-dollar mass under her armpit. More disturbing was that she had chewed off the top half of it, exposing the inside of the growth. It appeared solid and had an obvious blood supply in its center, which usually indicates malignancy. I worried that it was a cancerous tumor. How had we missed seeing it before?

I have a unique way of intuitively testing for cancer; this mass tested positive. My heart skipped a beat. It was too late in the day to take her to our veterinarian. I would have to wait until Monday to take her in for a biopsy.

I don't treat cancer in humans as it is a medical issue that needs expert care. But with my Gracie, I was determined to do what I could to eliminate the exposed mass. While she reclined patiently on our patio, I administered a treatment. I then meditated with her to choose the best way to heal her completely, with no reoccurrence.

I put my hands on Gracie to tune in. I saw an image of the two of us going to a steep, hilly field above our house. She and I needed to find a spot to lie down on the earth together to absorb the sun's rays and gather nature's nurturing energy. We were to do this daily for ten days. I loved the idea of having quality quiet time together. I figured we had nothing to lose by embarking on this healing journey.

I leashed up Gracie for our stroll to the top of this field, utterly overgrown with Manzanita bushes and tall grasses. A short trail angled downhill to a small clearing where we could just barely fit our reclining bodies. Gracie, timid in nature, was not too sure about this healing venture, but my coaxing and reassurance convinced her to follow me down to this well-hidden spot. I convinced her to lie down in the dirt ("Mamma, what?"), and settle in for a 15-minute meditation and healing session. I allowed my inner guidance to dictate our quiet time together. Within moments, we fell into a silent reverie, enjoying the warm rays of the late afternoon sun. I held her paw with a light touch. Within a few minutes, Gracie was out like a light.

We lay upon the earth, eyes closed, experiencing a gentle healing from the sun. Nature swarmed around us. Birds warbled, bees buzzed around the wildflowers, and the earthy smells of that field attuned us to life's healing process. After fifteen minutes, I felt our session was complete, so we rose to mindfully amble home. I felt attuned to Gracie in a new way; what a gentle soul.

I repeated this ritual with Gracie on Sunday afternoon and Monday morning before taking her to the vet's office. The tumor appeared to have changed. Did I imagine it? The vet looked at the opened-up mass with the blood supply and stated it was probably cancer. She extracted a tissue sample to send to the lab and said she would have the results by Wednesday.

Gracie and I continued our ritual of going to our healing spot. Our meditations were profound and nurturing. I looked forward to our sessions; it seemed my Gracie did as well.

On Wednesday, we got a call from the vet. She said that the tissue was not cancerous; in fact, they could not tell exactly what it was. She relayed that the tissue seemed to be in a transitional state, neither healthy nor cancerous. This was an affirmation that our healing process was working!

Then something miraculous happened Thursday morning. When I examined Gracie's tumor, I nearly fell over. The growth was notably smaller, now the size of a quarter. I felt excited; our process was working! Encouraged, we made our way up the hill again. Gracie seemed to trust me with her heart now, and my love for her deepened.

On Friday, the tumor was the size of a nickel. Saturday, it was the size of a penny, and by the next day, the size of a dime. Each day after that, it was reduced in size by half. My eyes could barely believe the miracle of healing I was witnessing daily.

By day nine, it was the size of a pea. The blood supply had vanished, and the hair around where the growth had been, mysteriously grew back. With most injuries to a dog's coat, this is not the case.

On the final day of our process, we serenely made our way up the road for our last commune with Mother Nature. We crawled under the overhang of our favorite Manzanita bush and quietly contemplated the journey we had just experienced. I could sense that Gracie somehow understood what we had been doing. She seemed to join me in giving thanks. There was nothing more to receive from the sun, the earth, and our guidance. We sat, breathing evenly with a quiet gratitude for the miracle of healing.

I ceremoniously made my way to Gracie's dog bed the following morning to check on the patient. With her permission, I lifted her arm to observe the results of our ten-day healing process. Despite our daily positive results, I was astonished that the tumor was completely gone, with no remaining scar. I could barely believe my eyes. I was awed at the mystery of the Universe and how it can unfold—if we allow it.

I then knew that when miracles happen, we must believe, give thanks, and realize whatever lessons are available. Even more, in the face of difficulties, we must learn to turn inwards to seek guidance from whatever source we feel is divine and then follow it impeccably to the best of our ability.

The tumor never returned. Gracie grew less shy and fearful as part of her healing experience. She lived happily for many more years, a joy in our lives.

This healing journey with my dear Gracie taught me so many things that I hold in my heart even today: the beauty of working together in any healing process, the power the natural elements offer us, and most of all, by working in this case, in a field, miracles can happen.

17

WHEN PETS ARE CHALLENGING

THE MEXICAN STREET DOG

Our "tails of the miraculous" would not be complete without our story of Carmela De La Luz. While vacationing in our favorite Mexican beach town, I noticed a gaggle of puppies hunkering down around a mamma about their size. My eye caught one puppy, a caramel-colored shorthaired scrub of a dog with Dobby ears and a thin, wagging tail. I swooped in for a pet.

I scooped up the Dobby creature and held her to my cheek as scrummy and enthusiastic kisses ensued. I was instantly in love and begged my better half, "Can we take her home?" I named her Carmela for her caramel coloring. Equally delicious. We were eventually persuaded to bring her back to the States to live with us. Even though I sensed this dog might be a challenge for us, I vowed to deal with it with love.

Her first moments in the USA were epic. I gathered her crate off the elevator that transported her up to the terminal. I hauled her to the baggage area to collect our remaining items. Who should arrive at that exact moment to get her luggage? Helena Bonham Carter. She was in Los Angeles to gather her Oscar for her role in

The King's Speech. "Is that a puppy?" she inquired in quite the British accent. We lifted Carmela out of her crate to receive her royal pet.

Our other dog, Gracie, had gotten used to being the only dog in the house. However, she graciously accepted this new arrival and even began to assume a matronly manner with the rambunctious Carmela. We now had two dogs, two cats, and a teenager living with us. We dubbed the whole enclave the Funny Farm, as there was always something to laugh about.

Emotionally, Gracie was my spouse's dog. She babied her, all 86 pounds of her. I was instantly attached to Carmela and proclaimed her as my doggie and then allowed to retain my choice of her name. This would include the subsequent nicknames of Carmie, Carme, Carmela De La Luz, Carme-Carme, and eventually D.D., which included a variety of meanings. She was cuddly, enthusiastic, and attached to Gracie, always following her lead. Sometimes, in late spring, we would hike in a wide-open park and watch with pure delight as the dogs sprang through the jungle of waist-high grasses and weeds. It warmed my heart to see both marching up the paths together, ears flopping and tails wagging with the joy of being in the high grasses. Carmie and Gracie would race down the steep hills, disappearing from our sight until we whistled and called them back.

On one spring morning, we descended into the lower fields of Parma Park, quite overgrown with tall vegetation, now fading from its winter's green. Carmela took off down a trail that wound into a canyon, hidden from our view. Moments later, there was growling, yelping, and screaming. Coyotes. Maybe three, from the sounds of it. My better half tore down the trail toward the commotion, frightened for Carmie's life. Suddenly, Carmela emerged out of the brush, coyotes fading in their pursuit. Carm had been nipped. She raced to us, terrified. She was alive!

But she was changed.

A year later, another damaging incident occurred. While on a higher part of the same trail, an aggressive Shar Pei, uncontrolled by his owner, lunged at Carmie two different times as I attempted to control the situation and included my shin in his vicious attack.

The owner took off quickly up the trail, no apologies, just as I spied the blood dripping down my leg. It took four months for that wound to heal. Carmie's easygoing spirit never did. She became a fear aggressor. While there were a few pooches that she trusted with her heart and soul, it took every effort on our part to control her around most dogs. She got away from me once and another dog walker as well, sadly, with vet bills ensuing. It broke my heart as I never had to leash my dogs until Carme. I so wanted her to be free to romp and spring through the brush as she had as a puppy. As it was, I had to take 100% responsibility for her actions. Sometimes, I failed in my job as the perfect dog mamma. It was a learning curve.

This inclination was what earned her the nickname of "D.D." or "Dragon Dog," for her sometimes-ferocious reactions to other dogs. I also wanted to think D.D. meant "Dear Dog" because she embraced humans with her heart and soul. Over time, I realized that Carme was my charge as much as she was my dog. I felt this in my heart and knew she registered it in her soul. She treasured my presence on family walks when I could make it. One move toward the shoe closet to get my hiking shoes was met with a barking display of joy, with her grabbing and tossing my socks into the air in determined exuberance. When I was her leash bearer, she was a perfect heeler unless we encountered small snarling dogs, of course.

Carmela loved her humans so profoundly that they could not help but love her back. She greeted each beloved family member or friend with a series of doggie sentences that let them know they were very welcome and, "Where the heck have you been? I missed you a lot!" Although our friends loved AhZha, many confided how much they adored "The Carme."

She connected to the Field by ardently wanting to be present at our meditations and classes held at home and in the OM Pavilion. She begged to be present in the room during our Zoom sessions. She seemed to sense the shift in the Field and, if not allowed in the room for the more focused meditations, would patiently curl up outside the door and "tune in."

DOGS HAVE REAL EMOTIONS

Gracie passed away just shy of her fourteenth birthday. Carmela de la Luz now loved being the center of attention. Because we were going to be traveling that summer, on a trip up to our cabin, we agreed, with great certainty, it was not the time to get our next dog.

The following day, my better half mentioned seeing a litter of Lab/shepherd puppies advertised in a local paper. "Ohhh! Can we go?" I said excitedly but then realized I was not to be trusted to see them--and not get one. Later, I spied another ad in a local paper promoting an adoption fair for stray puppies and dogs downtown. "We shouldn't go…right?" I said. We looked at each other. Pause. "Of course, we are going!" was her reply.

Yes, I was confused, but I decided not to argue. Getting to hold puppies: Yes! We jumped into the SUV and zoomed into town, scooting into a parking spot across the street from the dog fair. Immediately, I spied a prominent dog pen on the sidewalk that housed four small dogs. "Oh, no," I exclaimed. Sitting In the see-through enclosure were not only three older poodle mixes but also a sienna-tinted shepherd with a white blaze on her chest. With one ear up, one down, she appeared old enough to take home.

I sprinted across the street to the pen and scooped her into my arms. Soft and adorable, she showered me with kisses and nibbles. I was a goner. "Look," I cooed as I held her up, "This is the exact dog I was hoping to get. And she is the same color as Carmie."

My spouse tried not to succumb to my enthusiasm and had me put the dog back down as she pointed toward the back of the building where the more mature dogs were. By now, I realized that we were utterly ignoring our logical decision to hold off on getting our next dog. None of the dogs in the back was a match for us, so I pulled the better half back to the front dog pen. This time we took turns holding the puppy, who showered us with puppy love. People walking by were no help. "You should get that puppy. She is darling," they said. That was all we needed to slap down the payment for our new member of the Funny Farm.

Once we arrived back at the cabin, Carmela greeted the new puppy with suspicion. She was wondering what had happened to our big decision 36 hours prior. Not only was she less than excited, but I could also see that she was jealous and uneasy. So, I sat down with Carmie to lovingly clear her feelings of jealousy. Surprisingly, she soon seemed more accepting of the puppy. That night, however, Carmela whimpered and cried in her sleep several times. She was sad upon waking when she surmised that the new addition was still with us.

Again, I sat down with her and did a comforting clearing for her sadness. She perked up somewhat and allowed the puppy to rest her chin on her belly as we traveled the three hours home. As we drove, Carmie gave me the 'look' that she was doing her best to tolerate this sudden intrusion into her life.

The following day, I found her in my office, curled up like a small child in my leather chair, visibly depressed. She would barely look at me. I sat quietly with her and tuned in to her feelings. The message was clear: "Wasn't I a good enough doggie?" So, I did a third healing to address her low self-worth.

I then gently lifted her chin and looked lovingly into her eyes. "Carm, do you think we got that puppy for us? We do not need the extra work. We got that doggie for you!" She perked up, looking at me to see if I was telling her the truth. "Yes, Carme, she is your doggie."

With that pronouncement, she jumped off the chair and beelined for the living room, where the newly named AhZha was chewing on a toy. Without missing a beat, she initiated a playful motion toward her new sister. Within moments, the two were tussling over a stuffed toy and chasing each other around the room.

From that moment on, the two dogs became absolute best friends. Upon rising, they would kiss each other and, throughout the day, engage in vigorous playtimes after every meal. They ate and drank from the same bowl, never fought over treats, and missed each other if one left the house without the other. They even shared their favorite chair in my office, exchanging days on who got the first crack at ensconcing themselves in "Mamma's chair." Seeing two beings love one another so deeply was a joy for me.

Animals, especially domestic pets, experience real emotions. In this case, Carmela responded immediately when I cleared her feelings. This allowed her to understand my words of encouragement. Why? Because we were connected in our hearts, which is always the ultimate link to another in the Field.

CARM DEPARTS EARLY

Our pets usually live to be fifteen years or older. Carm became terminally ill at age twelve and a half. I felt as if I had failed her. After visiting the vet's office and administering several drugs and herbal remedies that did not work, the night arrived when we painfully realized it was her time to go. Her loving Funny Farm humans, dog, and cats gathered to memorialize her on her last night on the living room floor. She rested peacefully on her dog bed as we all shared how we loved our Carmela. At the end of the evening, she mustered the strength for one more walk, a slow parade through her neighborhood with all her loved ones. A dragon to the end, she even sounded one more bark-bark at a neighborhood dog that passed us on the street.

When we awoke at dawn to check on her, it was clear that we could wait no longer. Her beloved sister, AhZha, accompanied us on the journey to the hospital. The Funny Farm clan arrived at the hospital to be with her during her transition. Her heart seemed to burst with joy as we each hugged and kissed her one last time in the provided private room. Soon after, she slipped into the other world. So many tears flowed, yet we knew that Carmela's love would live on in our household.

The day after she departed this world, she appeared to me as I

was receiving an acupuncture treatment. This part of her story is a miraculous tale for my next offering. However, she let me know that she realized she was a challenge in my life and left our household early to make my life easier. This, of course, produced many more tears.

Throughout her life, I had many lessons to learn from my soul-dog Carme. Acceptance, patience, parental responsibility, and unconditional love were just a few of the beautiful gifts I received from being her mentor. I marveled at her ability to express joy, exuberance, committed loyalty, and even frustration in a humorous way. I will always be grateful for the love she shared with me and her many cherished humans.

18

AHZHA BECOMES A HEALER

HUMANS NEED LOVE TOO

Some animals are innately compassionate and inclined to share their healing presence with both humans and other species. We have been fortunate to have two such beings in our household. One was a wise and powerful healer, Sibalin the cat, and the other, our Shepard mix, AhZha. Sometimes I wonder if the cat schooled the dog in her healing ways, as AhZha was not always attuned to the emotional needs of others.

Healing gifts may be realized when the need of our loved ones calls them forth. So it was with AhZha. A treasured friend and caretaker of our fur babies dropped by one day. We invited her in for some 'catch-up' time. She sat in a chair beside the stone fireplace and looked down at her feet. When we asked how she was doing, she shared that she was suffering from a headache that was not going away. Listening to her tone of voice, I could sense her headache might have an emotional component. I wondered how we could help her.

Before I could offer comforting words, AhZha rose from her dog bed in the corner of the living room and quietly padded over to her. She paused in front of her 'sister' and then slowly climbed up onto her lap with her front paws to get closer. She gazed deeply into her beloved friend's tearing eyes, sincerely wanting to help her.

After a pause, AhZha gently graced her cheek with endearing doggie kisses. This tender gesture sparked a release of unexpressed grief that our friend was feeling for someone close to her. We nodded compassionately in support as AhZha continued to offer comfort. In time, our friend's sadness abated, and she felt much better. With her job completed, AhZha dropped to all fours and returned to bed. We all thanked AhZha for her healing ministrations. Soon after, our friend's headache subsided.

This was not the first time AhZha had used her compassionate heart to heal someone. Days earlier, I was ruminating about a loved one in crisis. I shared this with my spouse as we sipped our morning coffee. I felt sad for this person.

AhZha noticed this and got up from her dog bed to make her way over to my chair. She gently placed each paw on my lap, then raised them to my shoulders so she was looking into my eyes. She then kissed me on the cheek to comfort me. She did it with such heartfelt intention that within moments, my concern dissolved.

In still another of AhZha's administrations, the visitor was able to make an important decision that was weighing on her.

Thus, our dear dog earned her place in the family as the consummate emotional healer. She continued to intuit when a family member or a visitor needed emotional support, often appearing out of nowhere to offer comfort and solace. She has remained a joyful being who loves and expresses herself through playful antics. I love being greeted with her signature enthusiastic AhZha dance at the end of every workday, with a squeaky toy in her mouth and tail wagging circles in pure joy.

When we treat our pets as conscious evolving beings, we open ourselves to many lessons, the most essential one learning to love unconditionally. It is always a joy to encourage and support my pets' unique gifts. When I do much love comes back to me!

19

CATS RULE, RIGHT?

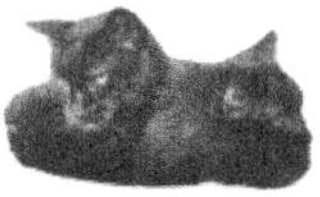

KU AND SIBALIN

One Christmas season, we decided to get a cat. Well, maybe two! We trundled off to the cat shelter to adopt the perfect stray. I strolled around the facility, peering into the cages, looking for my ideal cat. Sleek, black, and female were my criteria. I soon discovered that there were no cats to fit that description. There was, however, a rather scruffy, fluffy, stuffy black Persian female with aqua eyes who looked rather owl-like. She seemed sad, ensconced in that tiny cage. Her name was Tina.

The name alone outraged me. How could you name a black cat Tina? I knew I would take her home if for no other reason but to rename her. I brought her into the trial room, where we could interact with potential adoptees. She sat quietly and demurely on my lap and, within moments, was purring with contentment.

However, we also had laid eyes on a young, sleek black panther of a male cat with Egyptian golden eyes. As soon as he was brought into the room, he immediately jumped onto my lap to kiss Ms. Tina. We simultaneously thought, "Yes! They like each other."

The male quickly jumped to the floor to explore the small room, portraying his adventurous spirit. The female looked on with a certain serenity that was engaging. Did I want the responsibility of two cats?

It only took a few moments to relent. We decided that I would rename the girl cat, and my better half would get to choose the male kitty's name. When it was time to rid the Persian of her Tina appellation. I contemplated several mysterious names that might reflect the majesty I saw in her; none felt right. Finally, I asked her directly what she wanted to be called.

It didn't take long for her name to blaze through my thoughts: Sibalin. This name denotes the Mystery, as well as a famous historical oracle. Perfect for a black cat. She seemed to embody mystery and power and soon exhibited her psychic and healing gifts to humans and animals alike.

My partner had to ruminate on several iterations for the new male feline, such as Panther, Hadrian, and Spanky, with her finally settling on Ku after a Hawaiian god of war. He ended up being called Ku Ku. We even named the duo "the Ku Ku's." Even though Sibalin was three years older, these two remained a sometimes amorous and devoted pair until their end days.

KU AND SIBALIN FULFILL MY VISION

One morning, I drifted out to the warm sunlight in our OM Pavilion to indulge in quiet reflection after a hectic work week. I settled cross-legged on our wicker loveseat and emptied my mind of all thoughts. Soon, I dropped into blissful meditation.

Suddenly, an image of our two black cats flashed through my consciousness. In this fleeting vision, Sibalin was perched on my left thigh with Ku on my right. Both kitties were contentedly facing outwards, eyes closed and perhaps smiling. I enjoyed my brief rumination of co-meditation partners for a delicious moment, then chuckled my thought aloud, "That would never happen!"

Not so fast! Black cat magic was afoot.

Moments later, Sibalin strode into the OM. A petite "meow" announced her arrival. After my consenting nod, she adroitly sprang onto the couch, then meticulously arranged herself on my left thigh, pointing outwards. This was a first. How did she know to come? Hmmm, she might be psychic. We dropped into a deep meditation together.

Fifteen minutes later, a quiet thump landed beside me, followed by a gentle prodding of my right thigh. My eye cracked open just a slit. Ku was testing the waters of my outstretched right thigh with his paw. Without waiting, he leaped up, circled twice, and attempted to anchor his perch facing outwards. Not satisfied with this possible seat, he gave up and jumped down. On to some other imagined duty, I supposed.

Well, my vision almost manifested, I thought to myself. Sibalin and I went back to meditation.

Two minutes later, I felt Ku's paw again. My boy kitty was determined to join us in our contemplation time. This time, he circled thrice to find his perfect position on my leg. Once settled, he dropped into a contented purr session. After I processed my astonishment at their manifestation of my vision, we all enjoyed a blissful reflection of the miraculous.

When our meditation time was complete, my morning companions hopped down and sauntered off, leaving me amused and pondering the true origin of my mirrored-kitty meditation. Did I psychically call these two cats to join me? Did they dream up this maneuver, transmit it to me, and then manifest it to trip me out? Or did the Field insert the vision into our mutual reality to enjoy a quantum giggle?

I will never know.

CATS WHO HUG TO HEAL

One day, a patient told me that she was experiencing deep depression. I was concerned for her, even though she had outside support from friends and other doctors. I invited her to our

Saturday meditation group as an additional means of support through this rough period in her life.

I was surprised when she showed up for the meditation class. That day, eight students gathered, standing in a half-circle, placing my patient in their midst. We always began with a centering prayer before we would sit to meditate. Moments into our invocation, Sibalin hopped up the few steps leading into the meditation pavilion and strode right over to my patient with absolute purpose in her demeanor. She stood before her and looked up to assess what was needed.

To my amazement, Sibalin threw her kitty arms around the woman's legs in an apparent hug. She then rocked her from side to side for a few moments. I could barely believe what I was seeing. The woman just looked down, flabbergasted, and then giggled a bit. We all did. It lightened the mood considerably.

During the meditation, Sibalin jumped up on her lap, snuggled in tightly, and gave her the "purr remedy" with her focused attention. After fifteen minutes, Sibby jumped down from her charge to attend to her other possible household duties. When I suggested the woman stay after the class and rest, Sibalin returned and resumed her place on the woman's lap. She remained until her charge felt she was okay to drive home.

A more interesting thing occurred the following week. The woman returned for a second meditation class. As we all stood in our gathering circle, Sibalin again purposefully strode to this woman with determination. She threw her kitty arms around the woman's legs again, rocking them with an enthusiastic hug. This warmed the woman's heart, and we all marveled at Sibby's intuition and determination to assist someone in need.

More remarkable was that Sibalin recruited Ku, her kitty healer counterpart, to also offer emotional support to her human charge. Moments later, he bounded up the stairs and into the OM Pavilion, padding over to Sibby's charge. He threw his arms around the woman's ankles with added gusto, mimicking Sibalin's rocking gesture. We all enjoyed an astonished laugh at the two's antics before turning our attention back to the meditation matters at hand.

Perhaps most interesting is that neither cat ever offered a kitty hug to anyone again.

20

WHEN CATS ARE DOGGIES

THE WOULD-BE DOGGIE

One late afternoon, we enjoyed libations with friends outside on our stone patio. I sat on a wicker loveseat, taking in our ocean view through the oaks. My attention was drawn to the second-story windowsill of the front bedroom. There, Ku was perched on the window's small ledge and was surveying the property below. He then turned his gaze to our hospitality scene.

As a joke, I called out to him. "Hey, Doggie, come!" Ku glanced my way, paused, jumped down, then sprinted through the house. He sauntered onto the patio and looked over at me and tilted his head as if to say, "You rang?" I repeated my request. He bounded over, sprang up on the settee, and snuggled close, hunkering down for a delicious kitty nap. From then on, when I wanted him to do something, I called him Doggie.

Why did Ku prefer to be called Doggie? Perhaps he noticed our two dogs getting treats for tricks. Why couldn't he? He wanted in on the action. Soon, when I lined up AhZha and Carme for their treats-for-training, Ku would stroll into the room and take his place alongside the canines. I would ask them all to sit, then offer me their paw to shake. Doggie-paws were enthusiastically extended. Ku stood on his hind legs, then lifted his right foot toward me. Good Doggie.

THE WOULD-BE HUMAN TOO?

Perhaps this cat also wanted to be human. Through no invitation on my part, Ku discovered the joys of enhancing his palate beyond his assortment of Friskies meals. One day, while I grabbed a quick lunch before work at our antique oval dining room table, he jumped onto the padded chair to my left. He blinked at me with golden meditative eyes and his charming smile. He sat and appeared very Buddha-like. I was happy to have his company.

After watching me munch on some chips with my salad, Ku delicately reached across the table and demurely tapped my arm two times to let me know he desired a nibble.

"You want some corn chips?" I asked curiously.

His second tap-tap let me know, "Yes! I want some." After three or four crunchies, his palate was satisfied, and he jumped down to pursue other interests. I was so amused, I promised I would make a TikTok reel. But first, some rules!

First, no begging when guests were present and no paws on the table. Oh, and no climbing onto the table to amble over to a dinner guest's plate to have a look at their burrito—He tried that at least once. Over time, I realized he loved many salty, crunchy items: crackers, chips, and salted almonds, to name a few. He even favored the occasional cooked veggie or chicken tidbit. His gentle tap-tapping on my arm would continue until his appetite was satisfied. He then would sit quietly with eyes closed, no doubt giving thanks for the meal with his human.

Ku wanted to be included in many of our activities, especially when his loved ones visited. He greeted each visitor by jumping on their laps and kissing their third eye, always very gently. Close friends knew to call him Doggie to get extra kisses. He often joined me on the white, cushy couch in one of my writing surges, tucking in next to me with an encouraging serenade of rumbling purr.

KU UNDERSTANDS ENGLISH

Perhaps the name Ku inspired this panther-like feline to become a hunter of small things, including mice, rats, gophers, squirrels, lizards, and birds. This was a "no" in our household, with some exceptions. I sat him down and expressed my rules on hunting: no lizards, squirrels, or birds. I let him know that I greatly treasured these animals and that we did not want them exterminated. He intuitively understood me and then limited his hunting to rats and the occasional gopher as needed.

Several years later, the rat population bloomed after a particularly wet winter. Upon returning home after being away for two weeks, I entered the basement and was accosted by evidence of rodent presence. I was beside myself with horror. These varmints infested our basement, garage, and several outdoor structures.

I quickly found Ku and said, "Doggie, if you catch a rat, I will give you a treat!" I went away for two hours, and when I returned, he had caught a fat one and left it on the stone patio for me to view. "Good boy, Ku!" I heartily intoned. I went over to examine his catch. I was about to pick it up with a rag to discard it when I got a clear, intuitive message: "Leave it." I paused. Only a second passed when the rat made several squealing sounds, then squiggled away to escape into our stone wall. Ku watched with detachment. I turned to him and said, "Ku, you let it go!" He calmly looked at me and blinked. Still, he deserved and received his promised treat.

Later that day, I relayed the story of the rat that got away to a patient. She reminded me I had asked him to catch a rat, not kill it. Of course. He understands my English quite literally. So that afternoon, I went home after work and said, "Ku, when you catch a rat, you need to kill it." He glanced at me with some form of cat indifference; I could almost swear I saw him shrug his shoulders. I left on an errand.

I returned two hours later to discover Ku dining on the remains of a rat in the middle of the stone patio. I went over to view what was left of it. Once I had gingerly surveyed his catch, he walked away, having completed my request. Yes, he got another treat. Good hunter!

After seeing more rats in various parts of the property, I asked him to catch at least one varmint daily. To entice him, I said, "This time, I will give you the special treat!" I let him guess what that was going to be.

I came home hours later to a housekeeper having a squawky fit. She squealed as she quivered her hand in repulsion, pointing toward the dining room table. I peeked behind it to discover what was left of a rat. Ku was sitting outside the kitchen door, looking casually smug. Reward time!

Ku's absolute favorite treat was drinking water from a running faucet. So, as a "thank you," I called him into the bathroom. He jumped up on the counter, tracking my movements as I turned on a stream of cold water. "OK, Ku, drink up." As he lapped steadily at the refreshing flow, he flashed me the occasional glance with his kitten smile.

After that hunting feat, I rewarded him with this water treat whenever he fulfilled my requests.

Outdoor cats are decimating our songbird population. Their humans must do their best to prevent their felines from hunting and killing birds by keeping them inside whenever possible.

KU GETS IT

We usually removed the dogs' collars at night and sometimes threw them on a rug close to the front door. One evening, "Doggie" threw himself down on those collars. I laughed and said, "Ku-Ku, if you can put one on, I will give you a treat." He looked up at me, then began rolling his head around on them, attempting to get into one of them. "Pretty close," I said, laughing, and headed to the kitchen. Moments later, I turned and noticed that he was sitting by the treat cabinet. "Right," I said, "You want your treat anyway. Okay."

Over the following months, Ku practiced his trick. The nights he succeeded, he would proudly saunter around the house with the dog collar around his waist. I supposed he imagined himself to be a 'Big Dog.' He often slept on them, no doubt dreaming of his life as a real doggie.

KU DEFIES HIS DIAGNOSIS

One Sunday morning, Ku became very ill. I found him under a blooming camelia bush, curled up in the shadow of a shallow hole filled with leaves. He would not eat or drink. When I petted him, no purr came forth. I was instantly alarmed and saddened. I sat down under the bush to comfort him and offer healing energy. After a half hour, he appeared to revive somewhat and could drink water and eat a small amount of food. I knew, however, that he needed to be seen by our vet pronto. Fortunately, they had a cancellation that morning.

After the exam, the doctor told us that Ku had total kidney failure. This was a shock as he had appeared healthy for all his sixteen years. We were not ready to act on the sad options presented to us. In addition, we were soon leaving the household pets in our house sitter's care for two weeks, and I did not want her to be burdened with the final end-of-life decision.

Fortunately, one of my students knew how to treat kidney failure at home by administering a sterile saline solution. After watching a video, she coached me from her home via phone. Soon, I was administering his treatments every other day. Much to our joy, Ku sparked back to his silly, vibrant self. He grew to love the treatments as we would dance together through the house as I sang his doggie song on the way to his 'taking the waters.'. As a result, we grew very close.

Ku lived for a year and a half after his diagnosis. It was worth the extra five minutes of care every other day to stabilize his health.

He retained his loving and funny demeanor and was happy and sassy until it was his time to finally say leave us at seventeen and a half years old.

21

WHEN CATS ARE HEALERS

SIBALIN REVEALS HER GIFTS

I discovered Sibalin's healing talents from the various people that she treated. It turns out she took her job as a healer quite seriously. My first inkling of her gifts occurred after a young lady cared for our animals while we were away. She was recovering from a broken heart the night she stayed at the house. Sibalin insisted on perching on her chest, purring loudly until the sadness dissipated. The sitter made sure to tell us about her experience with gratitude and awe.

Over the years, I offered energetic healing treatments at our house. Quite often, Sibalin would appear during one of these sessions and jump up on the massage table. She could sense if the patient had an aversion or allergy to cats and avoided intervening. Sometimes, she would perch by the person's legs and purr loudly or, when invited, move onto the patient's belly, and administer measured kneading with her mindful intent to heal. I always enjoyed watching her work without expecting anything in return—a powerful lesson for all of us.

One might wonder: Was Sibalin an innate healer? Would she have offered her healing gifts in a different household? Did our meditation classes initiate her into the energetic realms of healing? Or did cultivating a healing Field on the property influence her proclivity to heal others? I often questioned the true origin of her talents.

SIBALIN MEDITATES

A few years after her arrival, Sibalin began participating in our weekly meditation meetings. At the beginning of the class, she would amble in, take a precursory stroll around the circle of seated meditators, and then attend to those she perceived to be in need by jumping on their lap for 10-15 minutes. The meditator would often pet her, itself being a soothing component of their healing. When she sensed they were balanced, she would jump down to pad around our circle to locate the next person in need. When everyone was attuned, she would find her seat and close her eyes to tune in to our meditation.

In later years, Sibalin would stride up the stairs into our OM Pavilion ten minutes early to find her preferred seat. As I walked in to set up for that evening's class, she often offered me a gracious "meow" as a greeting. Similar salutations were extended to the arriving meditators. She was an honored member of our group. This encouraged her to offer her healing ministry when needed.

SIBALIN HEALS BRONCHITIS

One night, someone in the group was recovering from bronchitis. She experienced a coughing jag that would not abate. This practitioner rose and headed outside so she would not disturb the meditation. Sibalin followed her out, looked up at her, and meowed, seemingly asking to be picked up. The ailing meditator lifted her and held her to her chest. Sibalin began her purr therapy. The coughing fit calmed within a few minutes. Relieved, the woman nestled Sibalin in her arms and quietly rejoined the group. Sibalin remained on the woman's lap until she was confident of her recovery. She then jumped down and left the room. For the moment.

Once the evening was complete and the students began to disperse, Sibalin reentered the room, heading directly to her 'charge.' She looked up at the student and meowed. She wanted to double-check and make sure that she was okay. With a laugh of recognition, the woman told her that she was fine, and Sibalin once again exited the room, satisfied that her duty for the night was complete.

This impressed the group member so much that she hurried over to me to relate all the salient details of her miraculous healing.

SIBALIN DELAYS THE INEVITABLE

Over the years, I have offered workshops to train others in my healing techniques. Just before a weekend workshop, a friend and patient told me she had not felt well for a while. She had consulted a well-known psychic friend who had "seen" a dark spot on her spleen. This concerned her. I had the intuitive thought to invite her to my upcoming class. Although she did not usually attend this type of workshop, she accepted.

The workshop took place in our OM Pavilion over a fall weekend. At our first break, I noticed my patient was on a massage table, tucked in under a blanket, apparently resting. I breezed over to the table to check on her. She saw me approach and sat up. I asked her how she was doing, and she said she felt much better. I presumed it was the healing techniques I had offered in the workshop and said as much. She corrected me, however, and shared that she had gotten quite fatigued during the teachings and found this unoccupied massage table to take a short nap.

She then related that Sibalin had hopped up on her table and, within moments, set to work, administering her ascertained choice of treatment. She kneaded her upper abdomen, covering every inch methodically. When that treatment was complete, she turned around and faced the woman's feet. She purred loudly for fifteen minutes. When she was finished, she jumped down and went about her business. When my patient opened her eyes, she felt considerably better, and the ill feeling that she had been experiencing for some time was gone for good.

Well, almost for good. Sadly, ten years later, the 'dark spot' returned to her spleen as a cancerous tumor. It was removed and treated, but then, as if it were her destiny, it returned with a vengeance. Within a few months, she passed. While we all grieved for her passing, I want to imagine that Sibalin provided her with ten good years with a loving husband, children, and grandchildren.

SIBALIN OFFERS SOLACE

For years, Sibalin preferred a hermit's life down in the bowels of the basement below the main house. We had to create a gate so that she would not live there and instead become a part of the household again. Nonetheless, she preferred the quiet of downstairs and was often hard to locate.

One morning, we invited a friend for breakfast who needed support. She was experiencing notable grief about her father, who was in the process of passing over. She struggled with whether to fly back across the country for the second time in recent months to say goodbye. We sat attentively with her to allow her to process her feelings.

As soon as we all took our place on the couch, Sibalin entered the house, padding by at the far end of the living room. Just as I noticed her, she glanced my way and paused in her tracks with a questioning look. I called to her, "Sibalin, why don't you come here and offer some of your healing energy? She needs you."

Without hesitation, she turned and headed straight to the couch where our friend sat. She stopped before her to assess whether to jump onto her lap or sit beside her. Sibalin seemed to know that she needed to assist this friend in processing her feelings. Up she jumped and nestled next to her. She modulated the rhythm of her purr therapy to quietly bear witness to what her friend was experiencing, matching her sadness with her purrfect attention.

Within moments, our friend was bawling her eyes out, expressing her goodbyes out loud to her father. She finally concluded that she did not need to journey cross-country again for a final goodbye. Satisfied, Sibalin jumped off from her perch, her healing offering complete. Off she padded to her original destination.

Once again, Sibalin exhibited her healing talents and ability to know when she was needed. This happened many times over the years. I often marveled over her intuitive nature. It truly expanded my perception of what was possible in animals when they were allowed to express their gifts.

SIBALIN STUDIES HEALING

I injured my right knee one year while hiking downhill with Carmela and AhZha. It was painful to walk for many months. I sought the help of various healers. One of them, a long-time friend and healer, stayed with us for a few nights. Whenever she visited, she offered me a healing session as an expression of her gratitude. During this visit, I readily accepted.

It was a cold winter evening in March when the two of us camped out on the rug by the warming firelight, catching up on life's circuitous journey. Soon, my friend began working on my sore knee. I closed my eyes to experience her caring touch. Within minutes, I experienced an encouraging shift in my knee pain.

Sibalin, then eighteen, was parked in her usual spot, on the back of the couch, facing the wall heater, in quiet kitty contemplation. As my friend worked more deeply, Sibalin, perhaps curious about what was happening, jumped off the couch, strode purposefully over to us, and positioned herself alongside my outstretched leg. At first, she appeared curiously interested in how this healer was working her magic.

But soon, she was entranced by these ministrations. She would look at my leg and then at my friend, observing her techniques. She offered 'meow' commentary and even seemed to ask questions. Sibalin's reaction to the healing process was more intriguing than what was occurring to my knee.

My precious cat left the room for five minutes but soon returned to her station beside my knee. I felt she returned because of some lingering questions she wanted answered. She gazed from my knee to my friend and back with calm concentration. I wondered if she was coaching my friend with her quiet meows.

This experience with Sibby affirmed my belief that any of us, including our animal friends, can continue to learn from others as we move through life's journey. After this incident, she seemed more committed to her craft, sharing it when called to do so for her humans and her dogs. This leads us to our next story…

SIBALIN STEPS IN TO HEAL CARMELA

As recounted in previous tales, Carmela, the Mexican Ridgeback mix, was an extremely sensitive being. She felt everything and often took the blame when her sister dog, AhZha, misbehaved. She was also very attuned to what I was feeling. It was emotionally challenging for her when I left on vacation.

One morning, when we were on the East Coast, I received a phone call from our house sitter. She shared that Carmela was curled up on the couch, shaking for no apparent reason. Nothing she did seemed to comfort her. She then related that Sibalin had decided to help her sister Carmela. She appeared from one of her hiding places in my office, striding confidently across the living room. Sibalin jumped up on our relatively small coffee table. She situated herself in front of Carmela and began to talk in her cat language, with a series of different meows that sounded to the house sitter as if she were coaching Carmela through her fears.

Sibalin then jumped from the table to the couch, snuggling close to Carmie. Again, more meows, then purring. Carmela's shaking gradually resolved. When she was finally calm, Sibalin hopped onto the back of the couch and watched over her doggie to ensure she would be okay. Once confident that all was well, she jumped down, sauntered over to my personal armchair (which she had never sat in), and took up residence as the house healer for the entire day. Carmela soon regained her feisty nature.

I often wondered exactly what Sibalin said to Carmela.

I always marvel when animals attend to other creatures, especially other species. There are so many stories and videos of these occurrences. With some animals, there seems to be an instinctual drive to help other beings. We humans can take note.

SIBALIN HEALS AGAIN

Toward the end of Carmela's life, Sibalin was again called into duty. While we were visiting Carm's hometown in Mexico, she again experienced one of her shivering episodes. Our house sitter called to inform us that Carm was not feeling well. As she related the symptoms to me, I tuned into Carm. Something was not right – it was more than anxiety. I instructed the house sitter to put one hand on Carme's sacrum and the other on her forehead to calm her. I tuned in and felt an unhealthy imbalance throughout her body. While on the phone, I sent healing energy over the quantum. Then I had a thought: call Sibalin over to Carmela for her healing input. I mentioned this to the caretaker.

The house sitter turned to look for Sibalin, but she was already making her way to Carmela's bedside. She perched beside her doggie pal and quietly purred, wanting to do her part to help. Carme seemed to recover. Our healing kitty continued to do her part by staying close to Carmela. When we got home, Carme was doing better. I made a point to thank Sibalin. Although our Carmela only lived another month and a half, we were grateful to have that extra time with her, thanks to the care and ministrations from our house sitter and, our dear Sibalin.

SIBALIN CHOOSES HER END

One day, I walked by Sibalin perched on a daybed. She lifted her head and softly meowed. I stopped in my tracks, then gazed into her beautiful aqua eyes. She did not look good to me. I leaned onto the bed. "Sib-Sib, are you okay?" I asked. She offered a second faint "Meow." She was not feeling well. I asked her again if she was okay. She then communicated with me that she needed to go soon. I paused.

"Honey, I need you here a while longer. Can you please stay an extra year or two?" When had asked Rune, he had complied with my request by living an extra year. I could sense her cogitating my entreaty. Then, a simple "ye-ah" meow was issued. Two days later, she was back to her old self. She was now more than eighteen years of age.

We joyously celebrated her nineteenth and twentieth birthdays. We had never had an animal in our care live that long. She continued her remaining time in quiet reverie, watching over the antics of the household from the back of the white couch. When Carmela was experiencing her last night on the Funny Farm, Sibalin took her place by her side, purring her last song for her Carme. She recognized the heart and soul of her doggie sister.

Ten days later, Sibalin went blind. This was a shock to us, but it did not stop our Sibby from navigating adroitly through the house and doing her part to keep the balance in the household. A few weeks later, though, she told me she would be leaving us. This time, I acquiesced, knowing her spirit's job was almost done. She earned her right to pass with dignity.

She was becoming thinner by the day yet holding steady. I left to return to the summer cottage, leaving several pet sitters to care for the Funny Farm. Then, one night, as all three fur babies played in the living room with their favorite house sitter, Ku suddenly took a dramatic turn for the worst. There was no denying that he needed to go to the pet hospital. By early next morning, he had passed in their care.

Three days later, I returned home from the East Coast after several long airport delays. Once home, I walked into the bedroom to find Sibalin. I was shocked to see how thin she was. I gently picked her up in my arms, rocked her, and placed her on the bed as I settled in for the night after my long journey. She purred weakly as I petted her with gratitude for her presence in our lives. I knew it would not be long before she joined Ku on the other side. I eventually dropped into an exhausted sleep. At two in the morning, she determined her job as the family healer was complete. She blindly jumped to the floor to find her way to the living room. I followed her out to make sure she was okay. My last words to her were, "Sorry, Sibby, mamma needs to sleep because she has a big day tomorrow." I closed the bedroom door behind me.

The next morning, I rose to find her lying on her side, beautiful yet motionless. She had left us, no doubt, in the early morning hours. Although shocked and saddened, I was grateful she waited until I was home. Although losing a third member of our household so close together stung my heart, I was quietly thankful that she orchestrated her passing. I knew I had to provide her with a proper burial at home.

I needed something nurturing to wrap her remains in. My heart breaking, I reached into the dogs' towel bin. None of them felt right. Then my hand touched something that felt soft and worn. I grabbed a corner of it and pulled. Out came a scrunched-up, unfamiliar beach towel. I shook it open. A short chortle eked out as I shook my head in irony. In the center of this towel was a Hello Kitty image, with its iconic smiling kitty face. Perfect for my black Persian dignified beauty. I imagined her rolling her eyes.

With the towel in my arms, I closed my eyes and silently asked Sibalin where she wanted to be buried. Right, next to Bella, the other long-lived Persian female, in her garden spot. I carefully arranged my precious cat companion on her burial shroud. I placed an owl feather (we sometimes called her Mrs. Owl), a crystal angel, and some sage from our garden in her bundle, carefully arranging her body in a soft embrace. I went downstairs to our English garden to dig her grave. I located a beautiful six-sided flagstone to be her marker. I then asked the last living fur baby of the Funny Farm, AhZha, to accompany me downstairs for the ceremony, which she did dutifully. She owed it to Sibalin after all the times she had chased her into a corner with her loud barking. We lay her in a final resting place, and I thanked her for her healing ministry. I wept with grief and gratitude.

All the losses then piled up into a series of heart-wrenched sobs. Then, the house was too quiet as AhZha, and I sat to gather our wits about this new reality. No black ink dots perched on the edge of the couch. No humorous conversations with animals that pretended to understand me. And then, no Carmela, greeting me at the door, in competition with AhZha to get the most pets and the most laughs. I cried on and off for days.

But Sibalin was not going to depart without offering a sweet gift. The next day, I gathered up AhZha in my car and took her to a local wooded park. Here, six of her humans had planted oaks in Carmela's memory two months before. AhZha and I did our walkabout and headed back to the car. Something nudged my attention to look down. There, at my feet, was an owl feather. A faint smile crossed my lips. I imagined Sibalin saying, "This is to replenish your owl feather supply." I shook my head in wonder and appreciation as I took a deep breath and then let out a long sigh. Over the next week, two more owl feathers appeared, one on a tennis court and the other in the neighborhood. I placed them in a memory bowl to inspire the writing of these tales. I knew her shining spirit would live on in our hearts for many years as Sibby Cat, my wondrous house healer. She truly was my miracle.

22

FUNNY FARM NO MORE, OR?

CARMELA SENDS HER REPLACEMENT

Ten days after Sibalin was laid to rest, one of the Funny Farm humans sent me a photo and a description of a dog urgently needing adoption. Her owner was ready to give birth to a second child and could no longer care for a large, active puppy. Pictured was a Shepard-Doberman younger dog with large ears and an earnest face. I would not have given it a second thought as we decided—once again—not to get another dog for the time being. Then I spied her name. It was Carmela. I took a sharp breath in. Who names their dog Carmela?

After all our losses, was this the right time to add another pet to the household? Probably not. But did Carmela or the Universe have another plan for us? I awoke the following day with the thought, "Good to adopt this dog.'" Every time I closed my eyes to think about adding a puppy to our now pleasantly quiet house, I received confirmation in my heart that she would be a great dog. I was mystified at my internal guidance being so forward. Now, to present this possibility to my partner, who was still vacationing on the East Coast.

Over the phone, we agreed it was not the right time, yet…the name Carmela prompted us to give this pupster a chance. I procured an "Okay, we can meet the dog," so I set up a meet and greet scheduled a few days after my spouse was to arrive home. But first, she had to process not seeing our two black cats sprawled on the back of the couch. It was tough as they had been fixtures in our household for seventeen years. Four days later, however, we mustered the energy to drive to Carpinteria Bluffs to check out this puppy needing a good home.

The first thing I spotted in the back of a small sedan was a pair of large ears. Then she sprang from the back seat. I was shocked! She was huge. Six months old? Please, let her be older. We took a nervous dog on probably her first walk through a field of high grasses overlooking the brilliant blue of the ocean that day. She pulled, she strained; my arm's strength was soon expended. I reeled her into "heel" when I could. It was more puppy than I expected.

At the end of our walk, we sat together on a large rock to discuss this dog's fate. If we did not take her home, she would end up caged in a shelter. That would be sad as we could see her potential. Though overwhelmed by our initial walk with her on a leash, I felt we should give this beautiful yet large puppy a chance. But because it takes two people to make this type of long-term commitment, I left the final decision to my dear spouse. With doubt dangling in the air, she rose and strode over to the trainers to tell them we would foster the puppy for two weeks. I was nervously thankful.

It wasn't the easiest of transitions. Thankfully, friends who love dogs came over that night. One of them discovered that her collar was too tight for her neck. Carmela calmed considerably when we loosened it. One of the women fell madly in love with her and, with tears in her eyes, begged me to keep her.

A dog-loving friend loaned us an extra-large crate. It turned out to be the key to managing her vivaciousness, and our sanity.

Our other dog, AhZha, was unsure about this upstart coming to live in her house. We could see that she missed her Carme deeply. My partner was again headed back to the East Coast ten days later, which meant I would face three weeks of training the pup by myself amidst busy workdays. Yet, within six days, we took the big step and agreed to adopt the strong-willed yet loving new member of the Funny Farm.

Carmela II became Ki or Kiki or Sugar Belle, and we were excited to see her learn new things daily. Everyone who met her fell in love with her. At times, Ki was mouthy and wild. She wanted to live on our laps. She over-roused AhZha, and AhZha would have none of it. But she would also lounge quietly on her dog bed or curl up in her crate and just "be." She crawled onto my 93-year-old father's lap, and they soon co-regulated each other's nervous system with gentle conversation and adoring pets. He, too, fell in love with her, calling her a natural beauty.

Then there is the circle of "Carma" that was meted. Back in the day, puppy AhZha tormented Carmela I with her need to tousle and play rough. Now Ki was doing her best to keep her doggie sister entertained while learning to be gentle. I was in constant training mode. Then this message came to me after an exhausting morning walk: "This girl dog will be with you into your eighties. Patience. She is finding her way through her teen years." My heart understood and accepted this message.

Daily, Ki began to understand what was expected of a Funny Farm doggy. Most importantly, she readily displayed her open and loving heart and was receptive to all the love coming her way. KiKi was also smart as a whip. Day by day, she grew calmer. I, too, began to relax and be thankful that my inner guidance had not let me down. Observing any being's evolution is rewarding, and Ki's ability to learn quickly became a source of joy.

The story of the Funny Farm will continue for as long as its humans can consciously care for our resident four-leggeds. Just as Ki now learns something new every day, so do I. Patience, consistency, and a calm demeanor are some of my lessons; shared unconditional love is my grace-filled blessing.

I also remain eternally grateful for the tremendous love I have felt for and from all members of the Funny Farm, humans included. From them, I have learned that love is the connecting matrix of what I call the Field. This uniting element of the universe inspires me to love, more and more with each dawning day. My motto is now "live to love."

23

ANIMAL HEALING ON THE QUANTUM

STUCK IN THE ETHERS

One chilly spring evening, while we were snuggled up in front of a toasty fire with our four-leggeds, I heard my name frantically being called from our driveway. "Valerie, Help! Come quickly. George is dead!" George was one of our next-door neighbor's happy-go-lucky standard poodles. We rushed to the door to find our neighbor hysterical, barely able to tell us that she had come home and found her dog prostrate on the floor of her den, apparently having overdosed on her prescription medicine.

I tore down our stairs and up her two flights to where his body was sprawled out, tongue hanging to the floor. George looked dead.

I called his name and saw a slight twitch of his paw. "He's alive!" I shouted. "We need to get him to the hospital immediately," I asked for a blanket to wrap him in to carry him downstairs.

After carrying him down the steep stairs, we loaded him (and his mama) into our waiting SUV and sent my spouse and the neighbor off to the emergency pet hospital. I stayed behind to gather the remaining pills scattered over the bathroom floor. There were only four out of the 36 capsules left. This did not bode well.

The staff at the hospital did what they could, but the outcome looked grim. George hung on, albeit in a deep coma. This was the last thing our dear neighbor needed to experience in her ongoing fight against cancer.

Two days passed, with our neighbor visiting him for hours daily.

Suddenly, it hit me: people in comas have out-of-body experiences; perhaps dogs do. I immediately knew I should see if I could find George in the quantum field. I sat down and closed my eyes to tune in and see if I could assist this precious dog in coming back into his body.

After minutes of scanning the Field, I found what appeared to be the spirit of George. He felt lost and confused. I mentally called out to him.

"George! You have got to get back into your body!" There was a pause.

"I don't know how. Or where it is." George replied.

I thought about what to say next and hoped his owner was at the hospital.

"George, look for your mommy's smile. She is right by your side."

George seemed to understand and indicated that he would find her. We were in luck. His owner was at the hospital, lying beside him.

A half-hour later, after two and a half days in a coma, George succeeded in his re-entry task. Suddenly, he opened his eyes, saw his momma and weakly wagged his tail for her. Within an hour, he was up and walking and soon went home to his beloved pack.

When the hospital heard about George's remarkable recovery, they were surprised and jubilant. Within weeks, they created a commercial featuring a prancing George and his mother strolling through a park. I wondered if I should call them to share my experience...but who would believe me? The important thing was that George was back with his pack and lovely owner.

The most compelling evidence of George's experience was that he now had a more conscious look in his eyes. He seemed to track what was going on in his dog pack with more awareness. I wondered if he had learned something from his out-of-body experience. In addition, he seemed to know I helped him back into his body, greeting me reverentially whenever I would visit them. He lived on for many years, surviving his owner, who succumbed to cancer a year later.

Until then, I had never considered that animals might have out-of-body experiences. I could have doubted it with this case, calling it a joyful coincidence. However, my experience with George assisted me in helping three other dogs who were poisoned and lingered in comas.

FURTHER LESSONS ON THE QUANTUM

During one of our yearly visits to Carmela's hometown in Mexico, we strolled down the expansive beachfront to call upon well-loved friends. I was also looking forward to connecting with their sweet pack of dogs. In the past, when a year or two had passed, the three canines would fail to recognize us at our first meet-up. They would "announce" our visit with a frenzy of protective barking.

This time, as we approached the house via the beachfront, even though it had been several years, we received the royal greeting, especially from Phoebe, a black and white skrit of a dog with classic droopy ears. In the past, she had been shy and skittish around me. Over the next few days, Phoebe would run out to joyously greet us when we visited. It delighted me; she was my vacation doggie pal.

One sleepy Sunday afternoon, I received a frantic text from Phoebe's mama. "Something's wrong with Phoebe! She is having seizures and can't get up. Can you come and look at her?"

I closed my eyes to tune in to Phoebe's condition. Intuitively, I knew Phoebe needed to get to a vet, pronto. I texted this to my friend, and by a stroke of luck, a veterinarian could see Phoebe on Sunday afternoon. The doctor determined Phoebe had been poisoned. She was given shots and fluids and sent home.

I walked to the casitas later that evening to check on her. Although alive, she did not appear to be breathing. I was deeply concerned for her recovery. Then I remembered my experience with George. While there, I administered a healing technique to mitigate poison in the body. I sensed a clearing had happened. She was in a semi-coma state when I departed for home.

Back in our room, in the middle of the night, I awoke and could not sleep as I was worried about Phoebe. Remembering my experience with George, I wondered if she was out of her body and if I could help her get re-embodied as part of her recovery. I meditated on this possibility, expanding my awareness into the Field. It took a few minutes to find Phoebe's energy. When I did, I suggested she find her way back into her body. She said "No," that it "felt bad in there," presumably from the poison.

Moments later, I dropped into a dreamless sleep.

I awoke in the early morning light with thoughts of Phoebe. In my half-dream state, I searched for and again found Phoebe in the Field. I suggested that she try to come back into her body. This time, she was willing. I observed her do so, then fell back asleep.

We rose that morning and headed for our daily beach walk, passing in front of Phoebe's casa. She did not run out to greet us. I hesitated to inquire about her condition in case she was still in a coma. We continued down the beach. I set an intention for her recovery.

On our return, we approached the beach in front of the casa. This time, Phoebe exploded from the edge of her property and bombed out to greet us, her tail wagging vigorously. She bolted over to me, skidded to a stop, and peered up into my eyes, expressing relief and gratitude. She had miraculously recovered and was her vibrant self again. We were dumbfounded! I bent down to pet her and whispered how proud I was of her for making her way back into her body. From then on, we enjoyed a much deeper connection with each other.

COLLECTIVE HEALING ON THE QUANTUM

Just two days later, I received word that the other two dogs in Phoebe's pack were now experiencing seizures and were unable to stand. I grabbed my spouse, also a healer, and we immediately dashed down the beach to the casa to see if we could offer healing assistance.

Little Kenji was not doing well. Kenji had been to the vet and was heavily medicated. I sat beside her to administer my applied quantum healing. No sooner had I started working on this fawn chihuahua when the smallest member of their pack began having seizures. I gave her a treatment to clear her of poison. Fortunately, the smaller one responded quickly. Kenji, however, was not doing well. Perhaps a collective healing was in order.

I suggested to Phoebe's mama that we three humans should do a group healing on the two little dogs. We sat on the couch in the outdoor living room with the dogs nestled in their dog beds next to us. A few feet away, Phoebe was stretched out by the pool. She lifted her head and seemed to realize our intention to heal the other doggies. She sprung up, trotted over, and jumped onto the couch to snuggle close to me. She looked up at me and, with questioning eyes, seemed to ask if she could participate in the pack healing. I nodded yes and gave her an affirming smile.

I placed my hand on Phoebe's back to connect her to our healing circle. We all closed our eyes as I led the group in a clearing meditation. I could see that our conjoined energy was much more potent than when I had worked alone. Soon, the Field appeared to lighten, and I knew we had cleared the poison on the energetic planes. It might take some time for the result of our work to become evident. The dogs needed to rest.

As soon as we finished the clearing, Phoebe looked up at me with a question in her beautiful brown eyes. I thanked her for participating in our group healing. She then jumped down to return to her spot by the pool. Before leaving the casitas, I stopped by her dog bed and told her I was very proud of her for helping heal her doggie pals.

The next day, on our beach walk, who should come racing towards us, but Phoebe and her dog pack, healthy and feisty as ever. We were greeted like royalty with kisses and tail wags. I was dumbfounded and thrilled at the speed of their recovery. We continued to enjoy these pups' vivacious greetings whenever we visited, now feeling a special bond with them.

24

THE UNIFYING FORCE

THE MYSTERY OF IT ALL

Throughout my journey with many of Earth's beautiful beings, I have often pondered who or what orchestrated these experiences and the subsequent lessons realized. What mysterious force drew these magical interactions to my doorstep and beyond? Was it in my soul's destiny to become a healer? Did the force we call God bless me with not only these animal interactions but also the follow-up experiences that occurred when I doubted my observation? Was this force of connection the quantum field that calls for unifying all beings? Does this enormously expansive God celebrate evolution through all substances, beings, planets, and galaxies? Why did these experiences feel so good?

So many questions! I do not require that any of my queries be answered – yet.

That said, my heart is grateful for the mysterious universal force that led me to discover some of the secrets of connecting and healing on the quantum. The real mystery is how the Field itself guided this educational process. When engaging in the healing arts, I am led by the Field to see, sense, or feel the true nature of an issue's underlying cause. It is a constant learning curve. I sense the absolute intelligence of the Universal Oneness both as a guiding and healing force. For this reason, I remain its most earnest student, as a lesson learned is a blessing earned. Perhaps I have become a quantum whisperer, as these lessons have led to many healing experiences with animals, humans, and habitats.

However, the most potent healing expression I have experienced with humans and animals is simply: Love. Love unifies all beings when offered unconditionally. I believe the Universe/God/Spirit is Love, and animals, in their various manifestations, are often an undiluted bridge to this unifying force.

I pray that I will continue to learn from all my human and animal co-inhabitants on the journey through this blessed life. I hope you will also discover true joy in experiencing and appreciating this diverse natural world in all its wild glory. And subsequently, vow to take care of it.

It is up to us.

EARTH DESERVES OUR LOVE

I have shared these tales as a memoir of my journey of becoming a quantum whisperer or, one who influences reality by tuning into the Field.

Cross-species communication is possible. I am particularly enthused to share with others the importance of living in harmony with all those who grace this gorgeous blue and green planet with their presence. My greatest wish is to inspire you to regard all beings, human and animal, with conscious consideration. The rewards are tangible.

You may awaken your connection to the Field.

You may have wonderous experiences with animals.

You may develop a deeper connection to yourself.

Your heart will expand as the miracles unfold.

Were we all to engage with one another with open minds and kind hearts, we could genuinely return to Eden or … experience heaven on earth. Our dearly beloved planet is going through many crises: climate change, mass extinctions, population expansion, pollution, and depletion of precious resources. The human species has assumed domination over nature and its inhabitants. We are often careless and destructive. While many will proclaim humans to be the most important beings on the planet, consider this: Earth and most of its inhabitants have lived without our presence for millions of years. Most could live on without us.

We are the only species that uses our "intelligence" to destroy our beautiful home. My heart breaks for the habitats that are being sullied and demolished. The greed for money and power is pushing us toward the edge of existence. Our collective carelessness and selfish attitudes of entitlement are systematically destroying this precious gem of a planet.

How can present-day humanity come into greater harmony with Nature and its manifestations? One way is to realize our interconnectivity with all reality manifestations, large and small, via the Field. Contemplate for a moment the immensity of our Universe with its two trillion galaxies and then wonder at the diversity of the insect kingdom that significantly contributes to the balance of nature. It's mind-boggling. The more I engage with the natural world, the more connected I feel to the Universal force that creates it all. Isn't it time for humanity to expand its conscious consideration for the abounding diversity of all beings on the planet and strive to exist harmoniously with them?

If you find resonance with these stories of earth inhabitants, wild or domestic, expand your awareness to embrace those you encounter. They deserve your care and humility. It is a precious gift to live on Mother Earth.

The future is created by what we envision today for ourselves and our children. Align with the intention that we humans shift our consciousness towards a more inclusive acceptance and care of all beings. Perhaps ask what you can do today for the good of all. I am always humbled when I can genuinely be of service. It feels right inside my soul.

Bless you, and may you discover the bridge to the quantum field connecting you with all beings. Again, that bridge is love.

And, it is essential to remember: you are one of Earth's beings, so be sure to love yourself!

EPILOGUE:

LOVE THE FIELD AS ONE

ARE YOU INSPIRED?

Have these tales of the miraculous inspired you a desire to feel and sense the field that connects us all? Do you desire to hear the whispers of earth's inhabitants? Are you someone who has a great love for nature? Do you feel drawn to communing with animals in the wild? Are you hoping to now communicate with your pets on a deeper level?

Perhaps this is the perfect moment to stop and appreciate the wildflowers in bloom, listen for a bird call, observe the insects and lizards at your doorstep, or address your pets as intelligent beings. But how do you engage with the Field and its co-inhabitants to experience your tales of the miraculous?

First, believe it is possible! These shared tales illustrate the potential for connecting with our planet's multitude of life forms through curiosity, respect, and love. Open your mind and ask the Universe to offer you lessons in manifesting the miraculous.

Then, venture out into the natural world and tune into the birds, insects, and animals you encounter with an open heart. Meditate or sit quietly in nature to avail yourself of the Field. Send clear and respectful thoughts to the animals you encounter. Practice inner silence by releasing thoughts as they arise. Over time, this will reward you with a sense of the Field as a matrix of communion, healing, insight, and love.

Communicating with the animal kingdom in nature or your home can expand your heart, mind, and soul while imbuing you with a calm presence. While not all animal interactions are insightful, their presence may remind you to look beyond your life's mundane 'to-do' push. What a relief! As you open to the possibility of communication with all forms of life, you will, in effect, experience profound and endearing lessons that become blessings – for you and those creatures you encounter. Our ultimate goal as humans? To experience the Field as love – for the One, all creatures, and, for yourself.

Following are exercises that will help you to tune in and attune to the Field. My fondest hope and prayer is that these easy-to-follow meditations initiate you into the wondrous world of the miraculous.

Perhaps you will join me in becoming a quantum whisperer.

EXERCISE IN CONNECTING AS ONE

- Sit quietly and feel your inner essence.
- Shift your attention to the center of your chest and observe your breath.
- Relax and let your awareness gently move out in all directions.
- Soften your focus and tune into the living beings around you: plants, trees, insects, birds, lizards, animals, including pets of course.
- Expand your attention around you to include every living element of the visible world.
- Affirm that you are all of it: the flowers, trees, insects, animals.
- Affirm that you are one with the 99% energy between the molecules of the dense world.
- Realize that you are innately and intimately a manifestation of God, the Oneness. This directly offers you a feeling of connection with all of nature and the magnificent universe we inhabit!
- Find your inner silence. Releasing thoughts as they arise. Then, extend this silence into Nature's habitat. You may feel a tranquil presence connect back to you.

- Elevate your thoughts and feelings to a more harmonic level; as you do this, the Universe will shine back to you with palpable ease, grace, and love.

CONNECT WITH NATURE AS LOVE

- Sit where you can observe nature.

- Soften your gaze by closing your eyes halfway.

- Breathe evenly, perhaps a bit deeper than usual.

- Releaser thoughts, even as they arise.

- Sense, then connect to the energy field around you.

- Observe what shows up: a bee, bird, insect, or a charming four-legged.

- Be present with, and then connect to this being.

- Say, "I AM Love."

- Radiate love from the center of your being to your surroundings and all that you love.

CREATE A MAGICAL FIELD IN YOUR LIFE

- Recognize that all beings have a consciousness and intelligence that deserve our respect.
- Open your heart and mind to listen for communications from the animals in your Field.
- Look for the meaning behind synchronistic events involving animals.
- Speak to animals gently and mindfully, while visualizing your intention.
- Meditate with them in proximity and include them in your awareness.
- Respect nature and wild animals as a gift to humanity to be preserved.
- Know that it takes time to tune into the Field or establish one in a household.
- Be the love that connects us all.

Acknowledgments

I first and foremost love and acknowledge all the beautiful beings that have inspired my journey into the miraculous.

To my partner in life, so much love and gratitude for your encouragement and advice in so many ways. Thank you for the journey here and to all corners of the earth.

To my many human cohorts who have danced in these tales of the miraculous, love, and blessings. You know who you are.

Thank you to my editors, Artelia Ellis, and Amy Cale, for their encouragement and direction.

To the women in our writer's group – thank you for your inspiration, your critiques, your honesty, and, of course, the laughs.

Appreciation for my human teachers: Victor Frank, Ben Colimore, Rupert Sheldrake, and Carlos Castaneda.

Love and appreciation to my sister shaman, Mujiba Cabugos, for all our journeys into the unknown.

Deep appreciation to my parents, Bud and Faith, for their gifts of true love for me, our animals, and the great outdoors.

I especially offer love and gratitude to all Earth's creatures who have been a part of Nature's Dance, and our survival as humans.

About the Author

Holistic chiropractor, energetic healer, writer, artist, and songwriter Valerie Girard, D.C. brings her love of animals, science, and an evolving spiritual path to this current compendium of miraculous tales.

Dr. Girard is the author of Recover Quickly from Surgery, How to Heal in Half the Time. She has written, directed, and produced ten theater performance pieces. She is also a songwriter, producing and recording two albums with Moving Breath.

She founded The Immortality Club, an online meditation group with a focus on spiritual evolution and planetary healing. She is currently writing an additional memoir, The Quantum Whisperer: Further Tales of the Miraculous, as well as The Daily Encodes: The Path to Accelerating Evolution. In addition, she is writing a Greek tragedy and hopes to soon publish her collection of poetry.

She currently resides and practices in Santa Barbara, California. She may be reached at drvegirard@panharmonic.com or viewed at: YouTube@QuantumWhisperer.

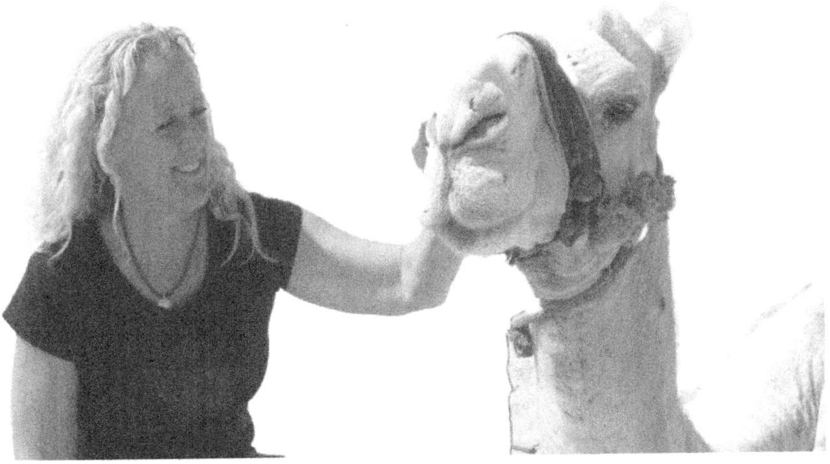

Made in the USA
Middletown, DE
28 January 2024

48154805R00109